52
L Simm
(Date - 1985)

KEN

A VISITOR'S

Published by Evans Brothers Limited
2A Portman Mansions, Chiltern Street
London W1M 1LE

Evans Brothers (Kenya) Limited
PO Box 44536, 48 Shanzu Road
Nairobi

Evans Brothers (Nigeria Publishers) Limited
PMB 5164, Jericho Road
Ibadan

Maps devised and drawn by Jillian Luff.

First published 1985

Printed in Great Britain by
Clark Constable
Edinburgh, London, Melbourne

ISBN 0 237 50748 X

KENYA

A VISITOR'S GUIDE

ARNOLD CURTIS

EVANS BROTHERS LIMITED

Contents

Maps

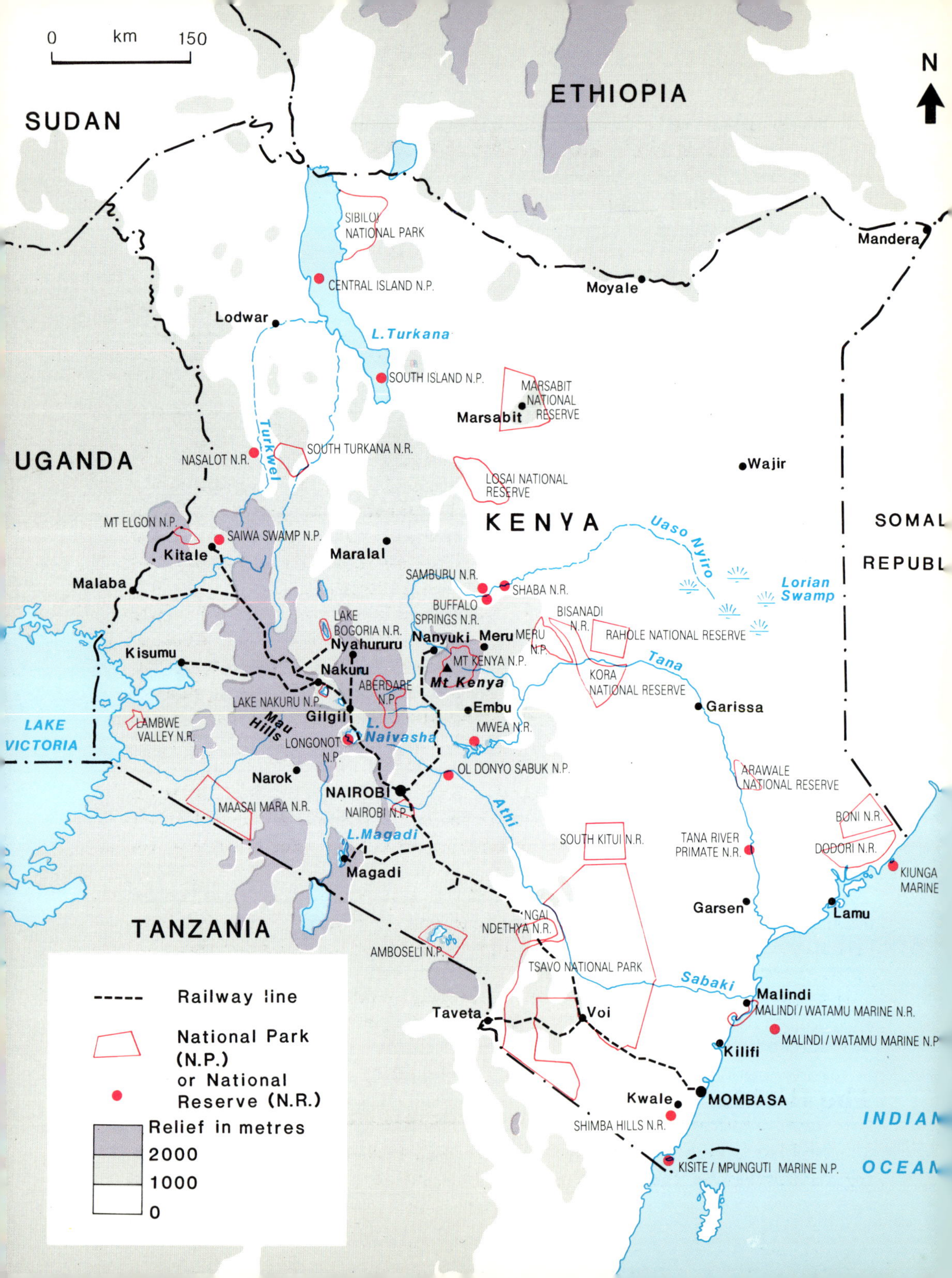
0 km 150
N
SUDAN
ETHIOPIA
UGANDA
KENYA
SOMAL
REPUBL
TANZANIA
LAKE VICTORIA
INDIAN
OCEAN
SIBILOI NATIONAL PARK
CENTRAL ISLAND N.P.
Lodwar
L.Turkana
SOUTH ISLAND N.P.
MARSABIT NATIONAL RESERVE
Marsabit
Mandera
Moyale
Turkwel
NASALOT N.R.
SOUTH TURKANA N.R.
Wajir
LOSAI NATIONAL RESERVE
MT ELGON N.P.
SAIWA SWAMP N.P.
Kitale
Maralal
Uaso Nyiro
Lorian Swamp
Malaba
SAMBURU N.R.
SHABA N.R.
BUFFALO SPRINGS N.R.
LAKE BOGORIA N.R.
BISANADI N.R.
RAHOLE NATIONAL RESERVE
Nyahururu
Nanyuki
Meru
MERU N.P.
Kisumu
MT KENYA N.P.
Tana
Nakuru
ABERDARE N.P.
Mt Kenya
KORA NATIONAL RESERVE
LAKE NAKURU N.P.
Embu
Garissa
Mau Hills
Gilgil
L. Naivasha
MWEA N.R.
LAMBWE VALLEY N.R.
LONGONOT N.P.
OL DONYO SABUK N.P.
Narok
ARAWALE NATIONAL RESERVE
NAIROBI
Athi
MAASAI MARA N.R.
NAIROBI N.P.
BONI N.R.
L.Magadi
SOUTH KITUI N.R.
TANA RIVER PRIMATE N.R.
DODORI N.R.
Magadi
KIUNGA MARINE
Garsen
Lamu
NGAI NDETHYA N.R.
AMBOSELI N.P.
TSAVO NATIONAL PARK
Sabaki
Malindi
Taveta
Voi
MALINDI / WATAMU MARINE N.R.
MALINDI / WATAMU MARINE N.P.
Kilifi
Kwale
MOMBASA
SHIMBA HILLS N.R.
KISITE / MPUNGUTI MARINE N.P.
Railway line
National Park (N.P.) or National Reserve (N.R.)
Relief in metres
2000
1000
0

1 The Land and the People

Look up Kenya in the atlas and you will find a country about 800 kilometres (500 miles) across from east to west, and about the same distance from north to south, though longer towards the coast, with the Equator running through the middle. Although it is wholly in the tropics, only the coastal strip has the sort of climate and vegetation which 'tropical' suggests to the northern mind's eye. Conditions in the rest vary, depending on altitude and rainfall.

The coastal strip has good beaches on the warm Indian Ocean, palm trees and casuarinas to lie under, and some good hotels. It is an ideal place to be warm and idle. For variety, sailing and deep-sea fishing are available, snorkelling (known here as goggling) in pools along the reef, visits to the Marine National Parks, some historical monuments of interest, and the occasional journey inland to the Shimba Hills or elsewhere.

It is the areas of medium altitude that offer the best game and bird safaris. This is where you realize that the wide open spaces are not just a figure of speech. However, little and often, or as often as possible, is the rule for game-viewing. If you stay too long at one time familiarity breeds a kind of indifference, perhaps increased by the indigestion that hours in a car without exercise may give rise to. But a return visit to a Park or Reserve is always a delight, however often you go.

When you visit a National Park or Reserve you should buy its map at the gate. These maps are not expensive. They not only give you the layout but also provide an account of the wildlife to be seen. Our book does not repeat the information which they supply.

The highlands offer the Mountain Parks, a chance to walk or climb on the mountains themselves, and the sports of a temperate climate. Those which are best catered for in Kenya are golf and fishing, and facilities for them get particular mention in these pages.

If, without rushing about, you can manage to combine these three types of vacation in a single extended visit you are much to be envied.

The Highlands

The highlands are the most productive part of the country. They are not very big, occupying less than a quarter of the land surface. Draw a line on the map from Mount Elgon to Kericho, through Narok across to Machakos, up to Mount Kenya, then back to Mount Elgon and you have the rough outline.

The eastern highlands, which include Mount Kenya and the Nyandarua Range, formerly the Aberdares, have two annual rainy seasons, the long rains from March to May and the short rains from the end of October to early December, and hence two seasons per year for quick-growing crops. The western highlands, including the Mau, the Cherangani Hills, Mount Elgon and Tinderet, also have rain from March to May, and still more rain on into July and August, thanks to moisture brought by the wind from Uganda and Lake Victoria, but they are fairly dry from October onwards. The stretch of the Rift Valley which separates the eastern from the western highlands is itself quite high, rising to around 1800 metres (6000 feet) at Nakuru.

The landscape has largely been formed by volcanic action. The Nyandarua Range has been built up by lava flows associated with the faulting from which the Rift Valley evolved. There are many craters in the Rift itself, including Suswa and Longonot and the caldera Menengai above Nakuru, with Lengai down in Tanzania still intermittently active. Mount Elgon is an extinct volcano. So is Mount Kenya, a much older one than Kilimanjaro, which is a geologically young mountain. Mount Kenya must once have been higher than Kilimanjaro, since its crater rim has long since been eroded away.

The Rift Valley

Kenya's Rift Valley is a small part of that great double scar on the earth's surface which runs from the Jordan valley in the north to Mozambique in the south. In eastern Africa it divides, the western arm running along the line of Lakes Mobutu, Edward and Tanganyika, and the eastern running through Kenya and central Tanzania. This eastern Rift is also marked by a line of lakes, from Turkana southwards to Natron and Eyasi across the border. All of Kenya's major lakes, except for Victoria and Jipe, are in the trough of the Rift. Some of them have fresh water, while others are soda lakes. It is the soda lakes which carry great seasonal populations of flamingoes, since they contain the algae on which these birds feed.

How high are the highlands? All of them are more than 1500 metres (say 5000 feet) above sea level, rising to the 4321 metres (14 178 feet) of Mount Elgon and the 5199 metres (17 058 feet) of Mount Kenya. They are usually warm during the day, especially if there is sun, and cool, if not actually cold, at night. Fires in the evening are welcome over about 6500 feet. This is a bracing and healthy part of the world to live in, and four out of every five of Kenya's 19 million inhabitants live here.

The Lake Region

Besides the coastal strip and the highlands there are two areas of medium altitude. One is the Lake Region of western Kenya, to the north and south of the Winam Gulf of Lake Victoria, with its hub at Kisumu. This is a warm, fairly fertile, well-watered part of the country which carries a sizeable population and is even overcrowded in some places, for example in Maragoli areas of Western Province.

All of western Kenya from the present border to Naivasha was at one time Uganda's Eastern Province, and was only incorporated in what later became Kenya in 1902. The lake shores in Kenya and Uganda have similar climates, and life is more relaxed there than it is in the highlands. The altitude of Lake Victoria is 1134 metres (3718 feet) above sea level.

The dry country

The other medium altitude area is the dry country, a vast triangle occupying more than half of Kenya's land surface. Its base runs all along the northern borders which the country shares with the Sudan, Ethiopia and Somalia, and its apex in the south is on the Tanzanian border quite near the sea—say 30 to 45 kilometres (20 to 30 miles) inland from Vanga. Over all this country the rainfall is insufficient for people to lead a settled life and practise agriculture except in isolated places—an oasis like Taveta, for example, or a mountain-top such as Marsabit. The critical rainfall figure in this part of the world is around 750 mm (say 30 inches) per annum. If you live where less than that amount falls, you are likely to have to depend on your livestock to survive and you are probably a nomad.

Round the edges of the highlands there is enough rain to produce good seasonal grass, and these areas, the 'grassland savannah' of the textbooks, are shared by nomadic pastoralists and game. Thus to the south of Nairobi you find the Maasai as well as the Amboseli and Nairobi National Parks; on the northern edge of the highlands the grazing grounds of the Samburu abut on the Samburu/Buffalo Springs/Isiolo National Reserves.

The further away from the highlands you go the nearer the conditions approach desert. There are patches of genuine desert, including lava fields, up in the north, but most of northern Kenya is better described as semi-desert.

The African peoples of Kenya

Kenya is physically a varied country, and the people who live here are equally various, since it seems in historical and recent prehistorical times to have been ethnically both a rendezvous and a melting-pot. Only in recent years has it become clearer how the three main groups of Kenya's Africans—the Bantu, the Nilotes and the Cushites—came to be in their present homes.

Far back in prehistory, eastern Africa may well have been of prime importance to the human race, since it appears from the work of two generations of Leakeys in Kenya and their colleagues here and in Ethiopia that this may have been the cradle of our species, the place where one of the lines of primates evolved into a creature recognizably man. A morning spent in the National Museum in Nairobi will give you some idea of the work done and the conclusions drawn from it.

The early human population of Africa south of the Sahara consisted mainly of hunter/gatherers. These were partly Khoisan (San is the polite modern term for Bushmen and Khoi for Hottentots) and partly Negroid, the former predominant in the south and the latter more numerous in the north. They have left plentiful remains of their stone tool industries. Most of these people have been absorbed by later arrivals, in Kenya as elsewhere, and the process continues today; but a few pockets of hunters remain, for example the Dorobo, a few thousand of whom live up on the Mau, and the Boni and Waliangulu groups of the coast hinterland.

The step from nomadic food-gathering to a more static existence was first taken by people who made settlements by permanent sources of fish. There was a period between about 9000 and 3000 BC when lake levels were much higher than they are today, not only in Kenya and Ethiopia but also in the Sahara, which was then green and fertile pastureland. There are sites of semi-permanent fishing settlements over much of the southern Sahara. One which has been investigated in Kenya is at Lowasera, near the south-east end of Lake Turkana; Turkana was then 80 metres (250 feet) above its present level and had an outlet into the Nile.

In time the inhabitants of the Saharan fishing settlements acquired domestic cattle, sheep and goats from the north and kept large herds, as rock paintings show. They must also have experimented with the growing of crops. The sources of such African food plants as sorghum and various millets have been traced to the southern part of the fishing folk's territory.

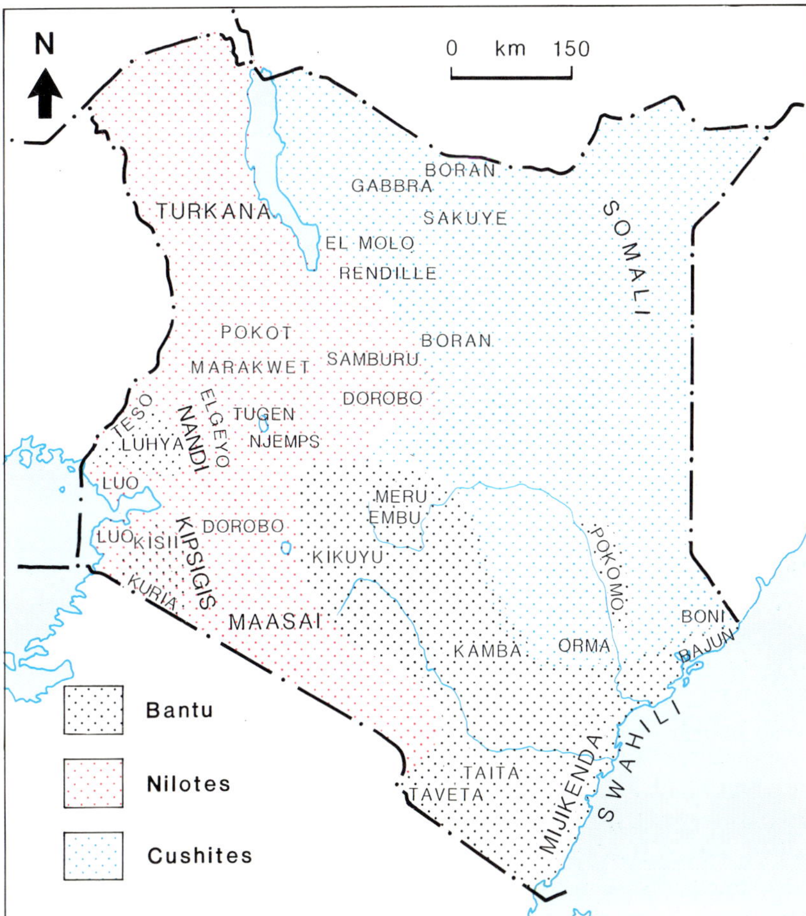

Peoples of Kenya

As the Sahara dried up in the third millennium BC migrations took place, no doubt over a long period, both to the south, into the savannah fringing the equatorial forest, and to the east, into the Ethiopian highlands. The beginnings of pastoralism and agriculture south of the Sahara are traced to these population movements.

It was from Ethiopia, probably around 2000 BC, that groups of Southern Cushites made their way south through northern Kenya, still at that time well-watered, via the eastern side of Lake Turkana to the Rift Valley. They brought with them the techniques of pastoralism, including the milking of cattle. Traces of their settlements have been found at Narosura, above the Nguruman Escarpment, west of Magadi, and on Crescent Island at Naivasha.

At some time before the beginning of our era these Cushites were absorbed or displaced (the modern Iraqw people of northern Tanzania are thought to be their remote descendants) by other migrants from the north. These successors were Southern Nilotes, a Sudanic people who were also pastoralists and users of stone tools; they are the ancestors of the present Kalenjin peoples—the Nandi, Kipsigis, Tugen and the rest—who now live in the higher parts of western Kenya.

The Southern Nilotic pastoralists were well enough established in the Rift highlands two thousand years ago to deter any settlement in their territory by the people who arrived next on the scene at about that time. These were the Bantu, bringers of the Iron Age to much of Africa south of the Sahara.

The homeland of the Bantu appears to have been on the west coast, in Cameroon, from which they spread out in two streams, one to the east and the other to the south.

The stream to the east moved earlier, probably during the last 500 years BC, through the savannah, north of the equatorial forest. It was presumably here that they encountered both improved methods of food production and the technique of smelting iron, thought to have already been passed on between the Sudan and northern Nigeria.

Before the turn of the millennium, this Bantu migration reached the area of the great lakes, where their sites are marked by the distinctive Urewe pottery. This was first identified to the north-east of Lake Victoria by the late Louis Leakey, who called it 'dimple-based'. The movement continued over succeeding centuries, until in due time it reached the hills lying inland from Mombasa.

The Early Iron Age site at Kwale, southwest of Mombasa, has been radiocarbon dated to the 3rd century AD. Remains of iron working, including some slag and a tanged arrow-head, were found there. Another distinctive style of pottery, Kwale ware, was found at and named after the site. It is widely distributed along the coast. Although Bantu of the Early Iron Age must be a significant ingredient of the Kenya population, they do not account for the

Bantu-speaking peoples whose names are now familiar. To trace their origins we have to return to the original Bantu dispersion from Cameroon and follow the second and later migration to the south.

This second Bantu stream in due course reached that part of Zaïre which was formerly Katanga and is now the Shaba Province. Here they multiplied and flourished in the second half of the first millennium AD. The more advanced economy and technology which they developed in that area were the basis of the cultures of the Later Iron Age, which spread with surprising rapidity over eastern and southern Africa in the early second millennium. The carriers, radiating from Shaba in the 11th century, formed another powerful wave of Bantu expansion.

These migrations included the speakers of the languages which became the Eastern Highland Bantu group, those now spoken in most of Tanzania and Kenya. As for the routes by which these ancestors of Kenya's present Bantu peoples reached their modern homelands, tradition suggests that our eastern Bantu group, including the Kamba people, the Wataita, and the Mijikenda round Mombasa, may have come via Kilimanjaro. The central Bantu Kikuyu, Embu and Meru, now living to the north of Nairobi, probably also arrived from the south. But some at least of the western Bantu (they include the Luhya, Gusii and Kuria peoples of Western and Nyanza Provinces) reached their present homes via Uganda.

As for the other present-day population groups, the pastoral Maasai, Eastern Nilotic speakers from the Sudan/Ethiopia/Kenya border area west of Lake Turkana, expanded far to the south in the late 17th or 18th centuries and came to occupy the eastern Rift Valley and adjacent highland grasslands as far south as central Tanzania. (There was probably also an earlier southward move of Maasaian peoples in the first millennium.) In the process they reduced the territory occupied by the Southern Nilotes. There were similar southward expansions by such related peoples as the Teso, Turkana and Samburu.

The Western Nilotic speaking Luo people, according to their traditions, left a homeland in the Bahr al Ghazal area of the Sudan during the 15th century and moved slowly east and then south towards northern Uganda and Kenya. They gradually occupied their present territory around the Winam Gulf and in South Nyanza between AD 1700 and 1900.

The Eastern Cushitic speaking peoples of north-eastern Kenya had their original homelands in southern Ethiopia. The area from which the Somalis dispersed appears to be the region of Lake Abaya. Speakers of some language ancestral to Somali and Rendille spread into the area between the Ogaden and the Tana and between Lake Turkana and the sea, perhaps in the middle of the first millennium AD. They expanded northwards to occupy the Horn, and then began, around AD 1300, the series of reverse movements to the south which have continued into the present century. Galla expansion from southern

Right: *Kikuyu children*

Below: Children, Kakamega District

Above: Luhya woman in Western Province

Far right: Swahili fisherman at the coast

Ethiopia is more recent, beginning possibly in the 14th century. Ancestors of the present Galla speakers spread through north-eastern Kenya and southern Somalia to the lower Tana, dividing the Rendille from the Somali in the process. They were a dominant force in north-eastern Kenya in the first half of the 19th century, but then lost their position to the advancing Somalis.

The non-African peoples

As for non-African Kenyans, the first to settle were the Arabs. Vessels from Arabia and the Persian Gulf had visited eastern Africa annually with the north-east monsoon since long before the Christian era, but they were trading visits only and the visitors went home when the monsoon changed. In Muslim times, the traders began to settle and townships grew up which were of mixed Arab and indigenous population. There is still an Arab element in the population. At the time of the 1979 census their number was 39000.

Asian traders, both Hindu and Muslim, have been established along the coast for many centuries. Their numbers were increased during the 19th century when Zanzibar needed to finance a growing agriculture and commerce. Another Asian influx followed the building of the railway at the end of the century, and during the colonial period their communities provided Kenya's main traders and craftsmen. Their numbers at peak were about 175 000, but many have emigrated to Britain and elsewhere since Independence in 1963. By 1979 the Asian population numbered 78 600.

Few Europeans lived in Kenya before the turn of the century, and settlement was systematically encouraged only in 1902 and later. Most of the European farms have passed into African ownership since Independence, but many settlers have taken Kenyan citizenship and have stayed on as farm managers or to take jobs in the public or private sectors of the economy. There were 40 000 Europeans in the country in 1979.

Facing the language problem

Kenya, with roughly 70 mother-tongues on its territory, is an ethnic and linguistic jigsaw whose Government has a formidable task to turn the country into a modern state. The problem is being approached in a businesslike manner. For example, Kenya's major secondary schools and colleges are required to take a mixture of students from different parts of the Republic, in an effort to promote national integration while minds are still open.

Naturally, communication is a headache, and some of the history of education in Kenya is a story of working out what parts in education should be played by the mother-tongue, by the *lingua franca* of Swahili, and by English. The upshot is that almost every educated Kenyan is tri-lingual, and converses fluently in his three languages, passing from one to another quite naturally, even in mid-sentence. English tends to be used most in the professions, in the upper reaches of business and banking, in hotels and at airports. A lot of Swahili is spoken in farming, in retail trade, and among the mixed work-forces of the tea-gardens or the sisal estates. Members speaking in Parliament may use either Swahili or English.

So what does a visitor do? He relies on English for most of the time. But he also buys a book and learns a little Swahili for emergency use in out-of-the-way places, particularly in the Bantu areas, where Swahili is understood more widely than English. If he is going to stay in one place for any length of time he learns at least the greetings in the local people's mother-tongue—local languages normally have a customary set of formal greetings to start a conversation. The use of these shows good manners and is usually met by a good-natured response.

Kenyatta Avenue, Nairobi

2 Nairobi and its neighbourhood

Nairobi is a pleasant capital with a population of perhaps 850 000. It is only as old as the century. If you think of a city as a big impersonal metropolis in which it is only too easy to be lonely and no one is his brother's keeper, you will find Nairobi very different. It is still small enough for local residents, black, white or brown, even those from up-country, to know a certain proportion of the people they meet in the streets. And if a handbag is snatched, which happens just as easily here as it does in New York or London, the citizens don't just pass by on the other side; they chase the thief and often catch him, and if the police aren't quick he may be beaten up.

The climate is most agreeable, with the mornings cool till nearly noon for most of the year, a warm middle of the day till 4.30 or so, and then a cool evening until it gets dark around 7.00. Parks and open spaces have been well laid out, the flowering trees and shrubs being particularly fine; jacarandas and Nandi flames are at their best from September to November, the pink bombax is flowering before the long rains, and bougainvilleas bloom for much of the year. The people in general are friendly. For a place of its size the city has a great deal of entertainment going on, much of it amateur but of high standard, and a lot of things to do. It also has a good variety of places to eat out, not all of them crippling in price.

Against Nairobi, however, many people would count its crime rate, which is high, a good deal of corruption (which afflicts African citizens more than visitors), a low general standard of driving on the roads, a bureaucracy that is ponderous and apt, especially in the lower levels, to regard itself as the master rather than the servant of the public, and too many sales staff in the shops who are slow and know neither their stock nor its prices.

Nairobi is right on the edge of Maasai country and has a Maasai name, which refers to its cold water. The pastoral Maasai in the 19th century used to come periodically and water their cattle in the Nairobi River, as they did at other water supplies round the edges of the forest.

Although the wooded area in the south-west of the modern Kiambu District was dominated by the Maasai in the 1880s, they were gradually being forced back by the Kikuyu. The Kikuyu people had begun an expansion to the south-west from Murang'a across the Chania River in the first half of the 19th century. A small group of kinsmen would negotiate for land with the Dorobo hunters who inhabited the forest, build their homesteads and make clearings for crops. Other groups would then leapfrog past them and set up other villages further to the south-west. As the frontier neared the Maasai thcy built fortified villages. The Kikuyu had reached the Nairobi area by this process of colonization about 1890, and were also beginning to use the Nairobi River for their cattle, when a series of natural disasters struck Kikuyu and Maasai alike.

In 1889–90 an epidemic of rinderpest carried off a large part of the herds of both peoples. In addition to this, Sir Frederick Jackson recorded in 1890, 'locusts had recently devastated the country'. Then in 1892–3 came a severe outbreak of smallpox which may have reduced the Maasai population by half. The survivors of the local Maasai appealed to the Kikuyu for help, and many were allowed to take refuge around Kabete, though the Kikuyu themselves were suffering badly; eventually the refugees were allowed by Francis Hall of the Imperial British East Africa Company to settle within the compound of Fort Smith, the station which the company had recently built there. The last straw was in 1898–9, when three rains failed in a row and the Kikuyu suffered the last of the great famines.

In the course of this disastrous decade, fresh Kikuyu settlement virtually stopped and many families temporarily abandoned their holdings and went to live with kinsmen in Murang'a, leaving only caretakers behind. Thus the new colonial administration which had taken over from the company in 1895 found southern Kiambu very thinly populated. It had no hesitation in taking

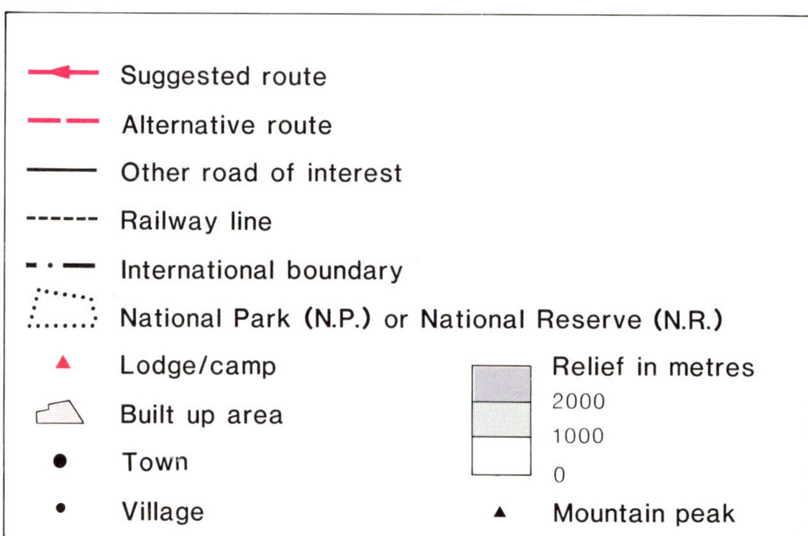

Key to route maps

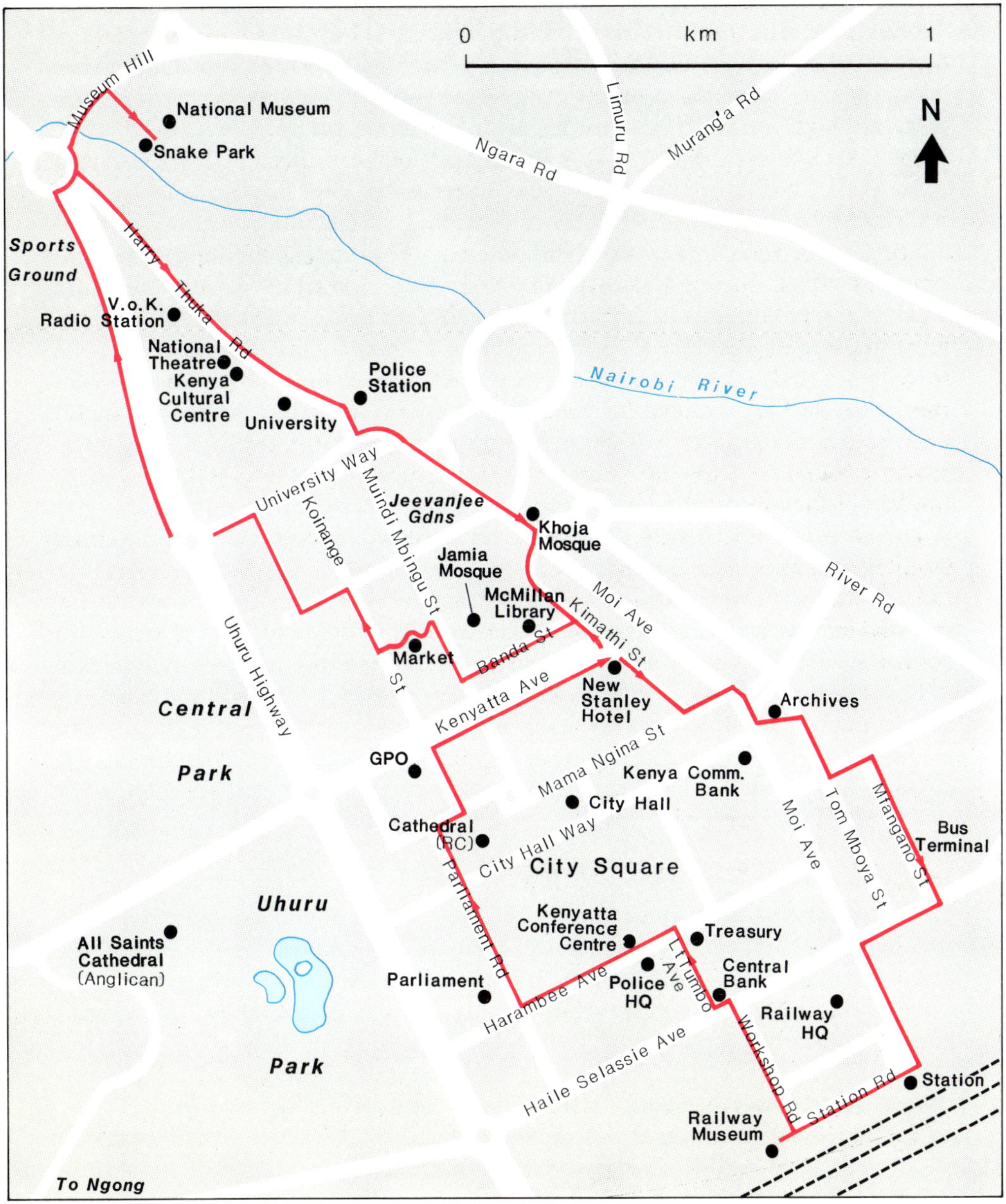

Nairobi street map

unoccupied and apparently ownerless land for European settlement from 1902 onwards, thus unintentionally providing ammunition for the nationalists who were to come. But the withdrawal of the Kikuyu did at least have the effect of providing the future capital with its green belt; the Kiambu Forest, the Karura Forest, the City Park, the Ngong Road Forest and the Dagoretti Forest indicate the high-water mark of 19th century Kikuyu expansion.

The foundation of Nairobi was incidental to the building of the Uganda Railway. The line did not actually reach here until 1899, but from 1896 there was a transport depot with stables for oxen and mules. This became railhead for a time while the engineers worked on the ascent into the highlands beyond. Ronald Preston, one of the assistant engineers, described it as a 'swampy stretch of soppy landscape, devoid of human habitation of any sort, the resort of thousands of wild animals'. However, during 1899 the Chief Engineer, George Whitehouse, moved his staff and the railway workshops to this site. John Ainsworth, the Government's administrator for the area, moved his provincial headquarters here from Machakos. Indian traders began to develop the bazaar, and Nairobi was launched.

In those early days Nairobi was less than impressive. Some gum trees were planted on the hitherto treeless plain and a street plan was made, but the town was dirty, full of dust in the dry season and mud in the rains. Plague broke out in 1902 and the Medical Officer of Health had everything burnt down, but it soon started up again. The first hotel was Wood's Hotel, a tin-roofed structure near the station on Victoria Street, now called Tom Mboya Street, which was the main thoroughfare. The Norfolk was started down beyond the bazaar in 1907. Some of the old wood and iron Nairobi buildings survive at the time of writing, for example the offices used by the Survey Department at the north end of Moi Avenue, next to the Central Police Station. They are built on piles, with a layer of tin to keep out termites; the floors creak, but the buildings are pleasant and cool to work in. The story is that they were scheduled for demolition and replacement in 1912.

A few buildings in permanent materials remain from before the First World War. One of them is the old DC's (District Commissioner's) office, now officially preserved, which stands on the corner where Kenyatta Avenue crosses the Uhuru Highway; it is dwarfed by the new Provincial Administration building behind.

Several buildings of better than average merit, if no masterpieces, remain from the middle colonial period. State House, the former Government House, and the Law Courts are good examples of official British colonial architecture. Among unofficial buildings that deserve more than a glance are the Jamia Mosque, the McMillan Library, the Ismail Rahimtulla Trust Library, the old National Bank of India building on Moi Avenue that now houses part of the National Archives, and the Municipal Market.

With modern buildings put up since the Second World War Nairobi has been fortunate. At the time when development of the city centre accelerated, the first crudities of the glass-and-concrete-box era had been softened and colour was being sensibly used. The Intercontinental Hotel is an attractive building. The Hilton is almost as good, and has inside a fine sweep to its staircase and mezzanine floor. Parliament Buildings are pleasant and suitable for their purpose. Bima House stands well. Best of all surely is the Kenyatta Conference Centre, a really successful design; by day the colour is not quite right, but you can at least see the reliefs of John Dianga, the Kisii sculptor; brightly lit at night the place looks magical.

The safari operators offer a number of standard tours. A typical tour of the city starts around 10.00 a.m. and lasts about three hours, visiting the main places of interest. A four-hour afternoon trip takes you out to the Rift Valley escarpment and a farm in the Kedong where a resident team of Maasai dancers perform. Another four-hour afternoon trip visits the Animal Orphanage and Nairobi National Park. Yet another afternoon tour, lasting three hours, is to the Bomas of Kenya; this is a cultural centre about 8 km (5 miles) out of town on the Langata Road where a staff of professionals put on performances of traditional dances, authentically based if somewhat choreographed and tidied up in production; there are also homesteads, and arts and crafts of various Kenyan ethnic groups to visit.

This chapter covers central Nairobi by means of two walks for those who get the feel of a place best by seeing it on foot; each starts from the New Stanley Hotel, whose Thorn Tree café is still the principal rendezvous. Some day trips are then described that can be made from the city.

Central Nairobi south of Kenyatta Avenue

Turn right from the New Stanley's front door along Kimathi Street. Dedan Kimathi was the chief ideological and military leader of Mau Mau on Nyandarua, then called the Aberdares, captured in 1955, tried and sentenced to death, but now honoured as a national hero. At the end you reach Mama Ngina Street, named after the widow of Mzee Jomo Kenyatta, Kenya's first President.

Turn left past the Hilton and the African Tours and Hotels booking office in front of it. Cross over Moi Avenue; Tom Mboya, Minister of Economic Planning, was shot in front of Chaani's Pharmacy in 1969. Bear right past Stanbank House, leaving the big Kenya Commercial Bank headquarters across the road on the right. Facing you is the old National Bank of India building where the National Archives now keep their art collection.

Go round behind this building into Tom Mboya Street and turn right. The Three Bells restaurant on your left serves a good curry. The next main road you

Looking across Uhuru Park to the Kenyatta Conference Centre and Parliament Buildings

come to is Ronald Ngala Street, named after a pre-Independence Prime Minister; it leads to the eastern suburbs. The four large buildings ahead on your right are the Diamond Trust Building, the attractive Rahimtulla Trust Tower, Gill House with its four floors of small businesses, and Development House. However, turn left down Ronald Ngala Street for one block and then right into Mfangano Street. After Bible House you pass the head office of the Kenya National Union of Teachers, a powerful union that has hotel interests in western Kenya, and then the classical façade of the Ismail Rahimtulla Trust Library. Go straight on, leaving the city's main bus terminal to your left, until you reach Haile Selassie Avenue. The headquarters of Kenya's coffee is across the road to your left, but you turn right.

Stop at the next corner and look at the US Embassy across the road, a handsome and secure structure. Then cross over left towards the railway station. Leave the railway headquarters building on your right and make your way round it to the right through the station forecourt. The station restaurant to your left keeps a very fair standard. Leaving Workshops Road to your right, go down Station Road and find the entrance to the Railway Museum, which is very good value. When you have seen enough of this, make your way back to Workshops Road and walk down it to rejoin Haile Selassie Avenue.

Haile Selassie Avenue was a death-trap until the City Council put a fence down the middle, so to cross it you use the footbridge which starts from the Post

Office on the corner. As you descend from the footbridge notice the powerful Central Bank of Kenya building to your right; the sculpture and reliefs in its entrance hall are by Gregory Maloba, who also did the giant figures in the grounds of the Safari Park Hotel. Go straight on into Harambee Avenue by Lt Tumbo Avenue, named after an officer from the coast who distinguished himself in the Shifta War of 1966–7 and was one of its early casualties. If you turn right here past the Treasury you come to Bima House. New and Old Jogoo House, across the street to the right, are Government offices, with the Law Courts behind them. Your route is to the left, past Police Headquarters, with the Kenyatta Conference Centre standing well on your right. There is a revolving restaurant at the top of the Conference Centre tower, and lunch up there provides fine views of the city.

Proceed past the Ministry of Foreign Affairs, the Office of the President and the Attorney-General's Chambers until you reach Parliament Road. Across the street, half left, are the Donovan Maule Theatre and, next-door, the Professional Centre, which now houses the Phoenix Players. You turn right along the front of Parliament Buildings, past the statue of the Father of the Nation, with the open space of City Square on your right from which they start the annual Marlboro Safari Rally.

A visit to Parliament is worth making, but in order to make one you have to ring up and get permission from the Sergeant-at-Arms, who will have you met.

One of Nairobi's second-hand clothes markets

The Independence Seal is of interest. So are the fifty tapestries presented to Parliament in 1968 by the East Africa Women's League and hung in the Long Gallery; they provide a fascinating record of colonial Kenya in pictures, district by district, wherever there was a League branch.

Turn left when you leave Parliament Buildings. On your left at the end of an avenue of flags is the Mausoleum of Mzee Jomo Kenyatta. Ahead is the Intercontinental Hotel. Down the road to your right is City Hall. On your right is the Holy Family Cathedral, from which the Angelus rings out at noon.

Go straight on past the cathedral, right into Kaunda Street and then immediately left. The British High Commission is in Bruce House, down the first turning on your right, and beyond it in Phoenix Arcade further along the street is Cottage Crafts, the National Christian Council of Kenya's curio shop, which offers good value. On the corner ahead of you is the Nairobi miliary stone, a monument to L. D. Galton Fenzi, the Kiambu coffee farmer who pioneered the direct road route to Mombasa and founded the local Automobile Association. A left turn here would take you past the doors of the General Post Office and on to Nairobi Provincial Headquarters where the Immigration Department has its offices, then to Uhuru and Central Parks and the Anglican Cathedral. Your route is to the right, along three blocks of Kenyatta Avenue, formerly Delamere Avenue, until you are back at the New Stanley.

Central Nairobi, north of Kenyatta Avenue

Turn left when you leave the Thorn Tree past the main door of the New Stanley and cross Kenyatta Avenue. Continue up Kimathi Street for one block and turn left into Banda Street. You soon reach the McMillan Memorial Library on your right, where there is a useful reading room and a good African reference library upstairs. Behind the library is the Jamia Mosque, opened in 1926, successor to that built by Muslim railway staff near the station in 1899–1900.

Continue along Banda Street to the junction with Muindi Mbingu Street. Muindi Mbingu, otherwise known as Samuel Muindi, was an early Kamba nationalist who led the opposition to compulsory reduction of the scrub cattle population in the 1930s. If you went straight on here you would come after a few yards to the rear of African Heritage, where there is a café serving varieties of African food; the front of the premises on Kenyatta Avenue is a superior shop selling African craftwork. Your route is to the right, up Muindi Mbingu Street, to the Municipal Market.

Walk through the market, just for interest, and penetrate to the crafts market at the back, which sells good baskets. Leave this market at the far end, emerge on to Koinange Street, cross the road and turn right. Down the passage where Caltex House begins is Alan Bobbé's Bistro, one of Nairobi's better small restaurants. At the far end of Caltex House is the Airways Terminal.

Turn left at the terminal into Moktar Daddah Street, past Antique Auctions, and right into Loita Street. At the end on your left is the *Maendeleo ya Wanawake* (Women's Progress—a national community development organization) Building, where the Goethe Institute has its home. The Institute is a West German cultural centre whose programme of functions is worth watching. The building next door is the French Cultural Centre, which has a more elaborate monthly programme and houses a good restaurant serving the sort of food that Frenchmen are prepared to accept.

A small link road north will take you to University Way, where you see to your right the back of the university's main campus and Foit's fountain in the courtyard. Cross University Way to Vermont Hall, the Synagogue, and go left to the Uhuru Highway roundabout. On the corner diagonally opposite, a new Lutheran church occupies the site of the old 1910 St Andrew's Church; the present St Andrew's, the one with the tower at the end of University Way, has the old church re-erected in its grounds. To the left of this, just along Nyerere Road, is the Christian Science church. To the right of it and straight in front of you is the Catholic Chapel of St Paul. To the right of that, just up State House Road, is the United Kenya Club, founded as a multi-racial club after the Second World War; it provides eatable food and comfortable accommodation at reasonable prices. At the top of the hill beyond, before the State House grounds are reached, is a turning to the Arboretum.

Cross the Highway, if you wish by the tunnel to your right which was built to help university students get from their halls of residence to their lecture rooms, and continue northwards. To your left are the university sports grounds. Beyond the far end of them, hidden in trees and surrounded by buildings of the university's Science faculties, lies Chiromo, built by Colonel Ewart Grogan and once the town house of Sir Northrop McMillan, the rich American sportsman and philanthropist; more lately it provided a home for the British Institute in Eastern Africa, a centre for archaeological work. Across the road to your right is the Voice of Kenya, the local Government radio station.

The trees and plants along the Highway are a good sight when in full flower. The strip dividing the carriageways is carpeted with bougainvilleas. Among the more striking colours along the footpaths on either side can be seen the mauve of jacaranda, the yellow of cassia and the pink of bombax, depending on the season; the leaves of the rangy acrocarpus, normally an unremarkable mid-green, turn to bronze before they fall.

Turn right at the next roundabout across Ainsworth Bridge over the Nairobi River and up Museum Hill. The International Casino stands on the bluff to your left, with a small garden below it. This is an attractive secluded place to sit and have a rest, but is apt to be visited by thieves and con-men. So postpone your rest till you get to the National Museum, first right at the top of the hill.

For many years the late Louis Leakey was curator of this museum. Now his

son Richard has the job. Each of them has had the gift of keeping the place alive and part of the life of Nairobi; parties from schools are continually visiting, and there is an excellent service inside of trained volunteer guides who know the collection and will take you round or supply information. The museum is strong in birds, butterflies and insects. It has a section devoted, as one would hope and expect, to prehistory and local evidence of man's origins. There are displays of some of the artifacts of Kenya's different peoples. You can study local game by means of stuffed animals in cases painted to represent their habitat. Joy Adamson's series of paintings of Kenyan peoples is here. There is even a fibreglass model of old Ahmed, the Marsabit elephant who was specially protected in his lifetime by Mzee Jomo Kenyatta's presidential decree. Between the front door and the river is the Snake Park, well presented and deservedly popular.

Grouped round the main museum building are an Education Section; the Wildlife Clubs office; the International Louis Leakey Memorial Institute for African Prehistory, with a pleasantly informal statue of the old prehistorian himself near the entrance; the Herbarium, which has a fine collection of plants and will identify specimens for you most helpfully; the university's Institute of African Studies; and next door the offices of the Fisheries and Wildlife Conservation and Management Departments of the Ministry of the Environment and Natural Resources, where you apply for fishing licences: their address is PO Box 40241, Nairobi.

Retrace your steps down Museum Hill to the roundabout and turn left, taking immediately the footpath to your left. The Boulevard is a pleasant hotel of modest size that has a terrace overlooking the Nairobi River. Beyond the Boulevard gate the footpath becomes Harry Thuku Road, named after an early nationalist who was secretary to the Young Kikuyu Association in the 1920s, fell foul of the colonial government, and was exiled to Kismayu; there were riots along this road after his arrest which left many dead. Thuku lived to a prosperous old age on his farm north of Kiambu.

This time you pass VOK (Voice of Kenya) on your right and come to the National Theatre, designed by Dorothy Hughes, and the Kenya Cultural Centre, home to a group of organizations including the Conservatoire of Music.

Across the street is the Norfolk, one of Nairobi's nicer hotels; its standards are high and it is aware of its past without being stuffy on the subject. The west end of the main block was rebuilt after a major explosion on New Year's Eve at the end of 1980. This appears to have been a delayed revenge for help given here when Israeli aircraft landed in Nairobi for refuelling and medical assistance after the Entebbe Raid of 1976; the man who planted the time-bomb in Room 7 is said to have left for the Middle East before it went off.

Continue along Harry Thuku Road with the main university offices on your right and the Faculty of Engineering to the left, round the corner past the

Central Police Station and into Moi Avenue. The old wood and iron buildings of the Survey Department are immediately on your left. After the Salvation Army headquarters on your right are Jeevanjee Gardens, named after a well-known businessman and philanthropist of early colonial times. The gardens are much used by office workers and amateur revival preachers in the lunch hour. The rather endearing white figure on a plinth proves to be a statue of Queen Victoria.

The main turning on your left is Murang'a Road, your route out of the city to the northern suburbs, Kiambu, Thika and Mount Kenya. On the next corner is the Khoja Mosque with its clock tower, still very much in use though the Ismailis have built a new mosque out on the Murang'a Road. To the left is River Road, joining Tom Mboya Street; to the right is Biashara (Business) Street, which is the modern incarnation of the old bazaar. It is probably the best street in which to buy textiles.

Take the next turning right and bear left round Barclays Bank. You are now back in Kimathi Street. When you reach Kenyatta Avenue the New Stanley Hotel is on the diagonally opposite corner.

Nairobi to Naivasha

Turn down Murang'a Road from Moi Avenue, cross the Nairobi River to Ngara, then go straight on along the Limuru Road past St Francis Xavier Church. The open spaces and dry forest to the right are part of the City Park; the Aga Khan Hospital is on your left. Cross the valley to Muthaiga, a suburb rich in diplomatic residences, and at Muthaiga Minimarket bear sharp left for Limuru.

You now cross Nairobi's northern green belt with the Sigiria Forest Reserve left and Karura Forest right. Go up the hill to the Kenya Technical Teachers' College and pass the entrance to the headquarters of the United Nations Environment Programme.

At the far end of Closeburn Estate a coffee factory faces the trading centre of Ruaka, named after the river which down stream supplies the breweries on the Thika Road; the name in full, *Rui rua Aka*, or Women's River, is said to commemorate a Dorobo woman who used to collect a toll from travellers at one of the fords.

A thickly populated Kikuyu countryside of part-farmers, part-commuters is on either side of the ridge which you climb towards Limuru. After Kirongothi Road on your right there is quite a steep rise; the flat ground at the top just before St Julian's Lane, once part of Wednesday Knight's farm, is known to have been a camp site of Count Teleki and Lt von Höhnel, the two travellers who were the first Europeans to traverse Kikuyu country and who passed this way in 1887.

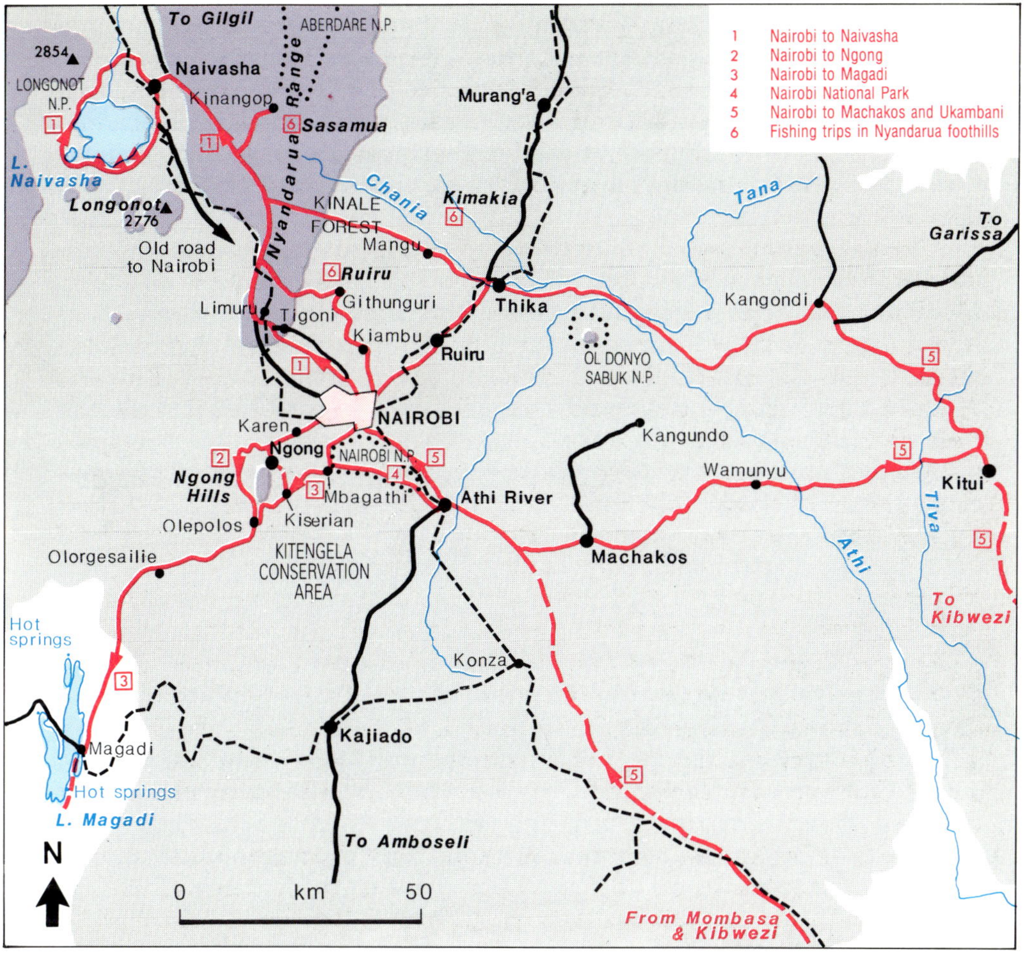

Environs of Nairobi

Continue climbing past the Tigoni turn-off and Limuru Conference Centre. Cloverdale Farm on your left was the site of Kiragu's fortified village in the 1880s, when this was on the Kikuyu/Maasai frontier. Climb the hill over the Limuru railway tunnel to 2250 metres (7400 feet) at the top, leave the turning to Limuru township on your right, and at the top of the next hill, 35 km (20 miles) from Nairobi, turn right onto the main road to the north.

Leave on your right the turning to Uplands Bacon Factory, 7 km (4 miles) north of Limuru. The factory was started in 1906 in order to help the newly-settled European farmers to diversify; up to that point the only crop with which they had had much success was potatoes. The first viewpoint over the Rift is reached 3.5 km (2 miles) further on; it has a wide view across Escarpment to Mount Margaret, Suswa and the Mau. The village of Lari is to the right of the road, mainly Kikuyu with a strong Dorobo component. This is where the Lari Massacre occurred during the Mau Mau Emergency, when a force from the forest killed nearly a hundred people who were regarded as collaborators with the colonial government.

The road continues to climb until it reaches 2600 metres (8600 feet) at the turn-off to Kinale Forest Station, 24 km (15 miles) beyond Limuru. This route used to be known as the Bamboo Forest Road, and the area was known as Mianzini, the place of bamboo, in the days of the caravan route; nowadays there are only isolated clumps of bamboo to be seen from the road. This was where caravans used to top up their supplies before descending into the Rift Valley, buying Kikuyu produce through Dorobo intermediaries who inhabited the Kinale Forest; the next source where food could be bought was the Njemps villages by Lake Baringo.

7 km (4 miles) further on is the fly-over marking the start of the tarmac road to Mangu and Thika, and 1.5 km (1 mile) beyond that is the second viewpoint at 2680 metres (8800 feet), with a fine prospect of Mount Longonot and Lake Naivasha below. From here it is a long gradual descent through ranching country, with patches of grey lileshwa and orange-flowering aloes, until at 54 km (34 miles) beyond Limuru you reach the right turn to the Kinangop and then the left turn into Naivasha township.

Take the Naivasha turning and go into the township, where you are now down to 1890 metres (6200 feet). There is a 9-hole golf course at the Club, the other side of the railway line. Turn left in Naivasha as though returning by the old main road to Nairobi, cross the railway and drive past the splendid stand of fever-trees to where the South Lake Road turns off to the right. Take this turning.

A visit to Naivasha is one of the most popular Sunday outings for motorized Nairobi, and at weekends the places where there is access to the lake get very crowded. The further round the lake you go the less crowded it is, but at the time of writing only the first quarter of the circuit has a tarmac surface and the rest is dusty and rough.

Like all the Rift Valley lakes, Naivasha has no outlet to the sea. But whereas Natron, Magadi, Elmenteita and Bogoria are soda lakes, Naivasha, like Turkana and Baringo, has fresh water. There are plenty of fish in it, the chief species being tilapia and black bass. To fish for bass, by the way, you need a licence, obtainable from the Fisheries Department next to the Museum in Nairobi. Boats can be hired from various places, notably Fisherman's Camp and the Lake Hotel.

As you circle the lake, the first place with accommodation that you come to is

Fever trees

the Lake Hotel. This is a pleasant spot at the water's edge with good thorn trees. There are full hotel facilities. Travellers used to gather here in 1949–50 when the main Nairobi–London air service was by flying-boat and the lake was Nairobi's terminal. Crescent Island nearby is a game and bird sanctuary, and there is Crescent Island Camp to stay at; in order to get there you have to be taken across a short stretch of water by boat. Another fully-equipped place to stay is the Safariland Lodge, also at the water's edge further round the lake.

Next look out for a turning to the left which will take you to the impressive gorge which the Maasai call *Ol 'Bulot*; the popular name is Hell's Gate. It is worth a visit. Lammergeyers, the big bearded vultures, sometimes nest in the high cliffs near the beginning of the gorge. There are steam jets at the far end. Not far away to the west are more steam jets, but these have been harnessed with the help of the World Bank to generate electricity and have become the Ol Karia Geothermal Project, contributing power to the national supply.

The next lake-shore stopping-place is Fisherman's Camp, which has self-help accommodation. The road then makes a detour round the so-called Inner Lake past Kongoni Farm. The Inner Lake is a former crater, but joined to the main lake. 5 km (3 miles) beyond Kongoni Farm, to the right of the road, is a small isolated lake lying in its own crater. This next stretch of road runs through Ndabibi, a large estate lying between the Mau Escarpment and the lake which was the home of Gilbert Colville, one of the better-known and more productive of the older European settlers of the area.

Look out for a large white house at the lake edge. This is the Djinn Palace, where the murdered Lord Erroll once lived. It is haunted by the ghost of Colville's dog, which usually appears on or near the anniversary of his death. The present owners say that when this ghostly dog on a ghostly chain appears, they are always struck by how cold it gets; for the duration of the apparition there is an icy chill. The small cottage up on the hillside to your left also has its mystery; many years ago a police officer living there disappeared one day without trace and was never seen again.

After Ndabibi comes Korongo Farm, where there is a very good camp site located under thorn trees in yet another crater. Take passing note of Loldia, the old home of J .D. Hopcraft, one of the earliest European settlers here; Loldia was the first stone house built round the lake; it dates from 1906.

As you leave the lake behind, you pass on your left the mountain of Eburu. The slopes were found to be very short of surface water, though well endowed with steam jets. S. F. Smithson, farming here in the early years of the century, tried leading the steam into pipes to condense and found he could make a tolerable water supply for his land. Eburu is now the site of a considerable settlement scheme. The road passes through a low gorge and then crosses the Gilgil River back to the main road. Turn right past Marula and the Malewa River to complete your circuit on the outskirts of Naivasha township.

Nairobi to Karen and Ngong

Leave the city by Kenyatta Avenue and continue up Valley Road. At the top of the hill turn right at the second roundabout onto the Ngong Road and past Royal Nairobi Golf Club. 6 km (4 miles) out of town, just after the attractive buildings of the Kenya Science Teachers' College, a Swedish aid project, fork left at Dagoretti Corner. The road leads past the Meteorological Department, Jamhuri Park, which is the Kenya Agricultural Society's principal showground, the Ngong War Cemetery and the Nairobi race course to Lenana School and the Ngong Road Forest.

Beyond the forest you are in the suburb of Karen, with St Francis' Church to your left. A left turn here would take you across Langata Road and past Karen Country Club, with its well-kept 18-hole golf course, to Karen House. This was the later home of the Danish woman who wrote that gracious book *Out of Africa* under the name of Karen Blixen. She was in fact the Baroness Blixen-Finecke, wife of a white hunter, and also wrote under the name Isak Dinesen. After she died in 1962, the Danish Government bought the rump of her old farm and gave it to Kenya as an Independence gift to serve as a Home Science college. The old house is kept much as it was. The college buildings in the grounds are now used mainly for the training of nurses.

Continue straight on past St Francis' Church and straight on again at the crossroads by the Karen shopping centre. After the next patch of forest you cross the Nairobi boundary at Bulbul, where there is a mosque, then reach the small township of Ngong 26 km (16 miles) from the city. There are a number of Muslim families living in this area. Some are the descendants of those Sudanese troops of Lugard's, the remnants of Emin Pasha's force, who were demobilized in Kenya. Others remind us that Ngong was a principal up-country staging-post for the Arab and Swahili trading caravans in the 19th century, and at points along the caravan route the descendants of coastal traders can be found. Ngong on the land route from Mombasa to Uganda has been compared to Cape Town on the sea route from Europe to India; its importance for obtaining supplies of Kikuyu-grown food can hardly be exaggerated, odd though this seems now. But in those days the forest edge reached almost to Ngong, and it was only as more and more trees were felled that administration moved north and east, first to Lugard's trading fort at Dagoretti, built in 1890, then to Fort Smith at Kabete, built in 1892, and eventually to Nairobi.

The Ngong Hills are pleasant to walk on, and still have forest in the valleys and some game, including buffalo. But leaving your car at Ngong may raise a security problem. One solution is to get a helpful friend to drop you at Ngong, then drive round and meet you later in the day at the southern end of the hills on the Magadi road. There are in fact roads or tracks round the Ngong Hills on both sides. The one on the east runs south from Ngong township and joins the main road to the west of Kiserian; it passes a memorial to Denys Finch-Hatton, an early airman who was a friend of Karen Blixen. The western circular road also starts from Ngong, but in a north-westerly direction, winding round the north of the hills, down into the Rift, and then southwards towards the Magadi road.

Nairobi to Magadi

Leave the city by the Uhuru Highway. Starting from Kenyatta Avenue you reach the first roundabout after Parliament Buildings and the second after the 9-hole Railway golf course and the old cemetery; at the third you turn right on the road to Wilson Airport, Nairobi's terminal for light aircraft. It is named after Mrs Florence Wilson, who started Kenya's first airline in 1929. On the right after the airport is Nairobi Dam, and to your left the Carnivore, a restaurant featuring its meat. Straight on up the hill leads you past the main entrance to Nairobi National Park and the cultural centre of the Bomas of Kenya. Turn left here along the Mbagathi road.

8.5 km (5 miles) after leaving Wilson Airport, you pass the Mbagathi Gate of Nairobi Park, 1.5 km (1 mile) later the Post Office training school on the right, and 1.5 km (1 mile) beyond that the left turn to Masai Lodge. The road climbs past the Catholic mission at Kiserian to the southern shoulder of the Ngong

Hills, and there is a spectacular view from the watershed at about 2000 m (about 7000 feet). From here the road descends in three giant steps to Magadi, lying at about 600 m (1900 feet) in the bed of the Rift Valley.

At the foot of the first step is the little trading centre of Olepolos, set in grassland with whistling thorn and other acacias. A further descent past barren hills to the right brings you to a broad plain, once a lake bed, where you see the sign to Olorgesailie prehistoric site on your left 67 km (41 miles) from Nairobi. The site was first noted in 1919 by J.W. Gregory, the geologist of the Rift Valley, and properly excavated by Dr and Mrs Louis Leakey in 1942–3. It is now a National Monument with a small museum. There are some self-help *bandas*, popular for weekend visits. The conditions are as for camping, so take all your own food, drink and bedding. Five stone cairns stand on the south side of the main road, on either side of the track to the site. They were excavated some years ago by Merrick Posnansky, who concluded that they were probably modern—19th or early 20th century—and Maasai-built, but not necessarily burial cairns. A defile below Mount Olorgesailie, following the course of the Olkeju Ngiro River where Maasai cattle are watered, brings you to the last gentle descent past a training camp of the General Service Unit to Magadi, 107 km (66 miles) from Nairobi.

Lake Magadi

The first sight of the lake comes as something of a shock. No doubt because of maps, one expects a lake to be blue, but this one is white. Most of the surface is composed of crystals called trona and forms a vast source of soda ash, used mainly in glass-making. The Magadi Soda Company has built a whole township on the shore, and a railway from the lake to join the main line at Konza. Soda ash is by a long way Kenya's chief mineral export. The company also produces about 40 000 tons of common salt annually for the local market. You pass the salt pans at the entrance to the township. If you turn left on the ridge up through the town towards the airfield you will find a sort of gazebo on the 9-hole golf course where it is possible to have a picnic in the shade and take advantage of any breeze that may be blowing.

There are some hot springs at the southern end of the lake. Beyond that it is unwise to take a saloon car, though there is a track of sorts southwards to Lake Natron. There is also a motorable causeway across Lake Magadi which leads to a crossing of the Uaso Nyiro River (not to be confused with the river of the same name in Laikipia). Pleasant camp sites under thorn trees can be found both to north and south at the foot of the Nguruman Escarpment, but the tracks are rough and stony.

Nairobi National Park

There are only 11 400 hectares (44 square miles) of the Nairobi National Park, but game is plentiful and its range is wide, including most of the species to be found at this altitude except elephant. Plains game is abundant, buffalo are usually here and sometimes rhino. There are always lions in residence. The reservoir which keeps the park populated is the Kitengela Conservation Area across the Athi River to the south and south-west.

To get to the main gate you follow the route to Magadi for its first ten kilometres and turn left at the park signboard. A useful introduction is a preliminary visit to the Animal Orphanage and the Conservation Education Centre. The orphanage is mainly a transit camp where orphaned or injured animals are rehabilitated before release back into the park, and their pens offer a good chance to learn at close quarters what the different species look like and how they move. The Education Centre has a small museum with models and shows films at weekends.

As for the park itself, entry by the main gate involves riding over a lot of anti-speed bumps. To see the full range of the park, turn back onto the main road and go out of town to the Mbagathi Gate. This opens into the higher forested area of the park where impala and giraffe are usually to be seen in the glades; it is a cool and attractive area not usually overcrowded.

If you specially want to see a particular animal the ranger on duty at the gate can often tell you what area to look in. The main points in the park are

Nairobi National Park, with Burchell's zebra, wildebeest and Maasai giraffe

identified by numbers on the map and on the ground, so you will be told, for example, 'the lions are at 19', which was probably true the previous evening. It is better not to pursue objectives in the parks but to keep to the speed limits and accept what comes. The more slowly you go the more you will see.

When you emerge from the forest into open grassland stay near the park's southern edge. Keep to tracks that follow roughly the course of the Athi River, making what detours you fancy to left or right. There are various places along the river—Python Pool and Leopard Cliffs, for example—where you can get out of your car and stretch your legs. Note, as you pass, the turning to Masai Lodge, a residential lodge with a fine position overlooking Kingfisher Gorge, but outside the park. Cross the Mokoyeti Gorge, where there are usually baboon. After the salt lick beyond, which lies between the park's numbers 14 and 11, there is a detour to the north worth considering—left at 11, right at 11a, and round the Athi Basin Circuit. At the dam on this circuit there are often Egyptian geese, marabou and yellow-billed storks, cormorants, black-headed herons and stilts.

Keeping to the line of the Athi River you shortly arrive at Hippo Pool, where you can leave your car under guard. There is a nature trail from this point along the river bank which is recommended. Hippos are often to be seen in the water and sometimes crocodile; one big old crocodile likes to lie up on a mud bank across the river from the trail's furthest point.

The track beyond Hippo Pool brings you out on to the Namanga road just south of the railway. Turn left and then left again for the 26 km (16 mile) run back to Nairobi.

Nairobi to Machakos and Ukambani

The Kamba landscape is warm and relaxed, and so are the people. The scenery is attractive but unspectacular. However, if you care to visit an African homeland where peasant farmers contrive to make a living in conditions of uncertain rainfall you will find Ukambani not without interest.

Go down the Mombasa road as far as the Machakos turn-off at 46 km (28 miles) and then turn left. Another 19 km (12 miles) past Potha and Katelembo, the old Percival and Hill farms, will bring you into Machakos town. The hill to your right is Kilima Kimwe, at the foot of which Masaku (or Machako), the man with whom the Imperial British East Africa Company negotiated, had his village. The Company's post was opened at Machakos in 1889, but the first commandant fell out with the local people and relations were bad until the capable John Ainsworth took over in 1892. It was Ainsworth who became the British Government's representative here in 1895 and who moved the provincial headquarters from here to Nairobi in 1899. A photograph survives of Machakos fort in 1899, but in about 1922 the DC had it pulled down.

In Machakos township the local market makes a colourful scene if you are lucky enough to hit a market day; at present produce is sold on two days per week and second-hand clothes on one. There is a new municipal headquarters, dignified but rather fort-like. The General Hospital has an impressive new out-patients department erected with West German aid. There is a Muslim population, as in Kitui and most townships that had a long historical connection with the coast, and the mosque is worth looking at; it has an attractive façade. There is accommodation at the Machakos Inn. The 9 holes at the Club are at present the only golf course in Eastern Province.

The Kamba people belong to Kenya's Eastern Bantu group and according to tradition their ancestors were living in the Kilimanjaro region in the 16th century. Towards the end of that century they began to migrate northwards via the Chyulus, Kibwezi and Nzaui, the sentinel peak called the gateway to the highlands. By about AD 1650 they were settling in the Mbooni Hills, a high, fertile area that was then thickly forested. It was from Mbooni that the people gradually spread out to occupy the present Machakos District, and from there also that parties crossed the Athi River, beginning in about 1715, to found settlements in Kitui.

For about 60 years, roughly from 1790 to 1850, the Kamba were the great traders of this part of Kenya, dealing in ivory, ornaments, skins and many other things between Kikuyuland and Mombasa; they were the recognized experts in making arrow poison. Links between Kitui and the coast were specially close. But Kwavi Maasai pressure in the mid-19th century and the insecurity of travelling parties weakened trade. When it revived again later in the century the initiative was in the opposite direction; it was not Kamba who then took goods to the coast, but Arabs and Swahilis who brought trade goods with their caravans up country and returned to Mombasa with ivory and slaves. Men from Ukambani still like to travel and traditionally they form an important element in the armed services and the police.

The road north from Machakos leads to Kangundo and the Kanzalu Hills, one of the more productive Kamba areas. The road to the south is the one you take for Mbooni and its sister hilltop demi-paradise of Kilungu across the valley to the south. Your route is to the west, out past the hospital and the bus terminal on the Kitui road. This leads via Masii to the village of Wamunyu, about 38 km (24 miles) from Machakos, which plays an important part in the local economy, since it is the headquarters of Kamba wood-carving.

It appears that there was no tradition of figure-carving in the old days. The craft was learnt during the First World War in Dar es Salaam by a Kamba soldier who taught his friends when he got home. Now these small wooden figures are produced in hundreds and appear all over the world; an occasional piece has individual merit. Meanwhile Wamunyu has expanded from a few homesteads to a fair-sized village; not long ago they turned themselves into a co-operative.

After Wamunyu the road descends into the valley of the Athi and crosses the river after 9 km (5.5 miles) on a concrete causeway. On the further bank you are in Kitui District, which is a little lower and drier than Machakos.

Beware of stream-beds in this kind of country, since they are liable to flash floods in times of rain; a bus was swept away with the loss of many lives some years ago at the Tiva River crossing, 25 km (15 miles) further on. 109 km (67 miles) after leaving Machakos you reach Kitui.

To return to Nairobi by the main road you leave Kitui by the route you came in but continue north-west towards Karati. The road eventually joins up with the Garissa road, and leads to Thika and so to the city. It is also possible, if you have plenty of time and would like a more unusual journey, to take the long road to the south out of Kitui and join the Mombasa/Nairobi road at Kibwezi.

Nairobi to the Nyandarua Foothills

The lower slopes of Nyandarua, formerly the Aberdares, extend almost to Nairobi. They provide places to fish within easy reach of the capital and some pleasant areas of forest.

To fish for black bass or tilapia in the Ruiru Dam, which belongs to Nairobi City Council, you first need a permit from the Water Department of City Hall.

Kamba wood carver

Your route is out on the Murang'a road as though heading for Thika, but fork left at the Mathare roundabout alongside Muthaiga golf course. You reach Kiambu at km 12 (7.5 miles) from the city (it has a good 9-hole golf course at the Club) and go straight on through the township as far as the 9-hole Ndumberi golf course, where you turn right for Githunguri. Githunguri is reached at km 14.5 (9 miles) from Kiambu, and you should ask there for further directions. The dam is about 3 km (2 miles) to the north-west, but the roads may be confusing. You can return from Githunguri to Nairobi by taking the road westwards to Kambaa, attractive Kikuyu country where a good part of the population is of Dorobo origin. This route comes out past Uplands Bacon Factory on to the main road northwards from Nairobi.

Sasamua Dam is also the property of Nairobi City Council and again you need a permit from City Hall before you start. This stretch of water, still a significant part of Nairobi's water supply, is stocked with brown and rainbow trout. To get there you proceed up the main road to the north from Nairobi as though going to Naivasha, but just before the second viewpoint cross over the fly-over and then turn left to Njabini, 21 km away. Ask at the police station in Njabini for directions to the dam.

A third objective for fishermen is the Kimakia Fishing Camp, which lies between the Kimakia and Chania Rivers in Murang'a District, not far from the border with Kiambu. The camp is run by the Kenya Fisheries Department on a

Kamba drummers and dancers

self-help basis. Further information is obtainable from the Fisheries Department next to the Museum, and it is wise in any case to check with them before setting off to fish any particular waters. The route is out to Thika on the Murang'a road, then up the tarmac road to the left directly opposite the Blue Posts Hotel in Thika. A left turn at the village of Gatura takes you across the Kimakia and a route continues up the ridge between that river and the Chania until the camp is reached.

If you are not planning to fish but would like a picnic and a walk in a cool area of highland forest that is uncrowded, turn up the White Sisters Road to the left just short of the Thika fly-over and then take the tarmac road from Mangu that leads north-west to the Kinale Forest. It rises to about 2600 metres (8600 feet), and joins the main Naivasha road at the fly-over just south of the northerly viewpoint. For a change of scene on the return to Nairobi turn left near the Manguo Swamp through Limuru township, cross the railway line by the Bata shoe factory and, keeping the railway on your right, make your way back to Ruaka and the city on the Limuru 'A' Route. A right turn at Tigoni Police Station would take you to Limuru Country Club and its 18-hole golf course. 11 km (7 miles) south of Limuru you will see Limuru Boys' Centre, an agricultural training centre for boys from poor families, and next door to it Kentmere Club, which has good food.

Places to stay

Nairobi

Ambassadeur Hotel
Boulevard Hotel
Excelsior Hotel
Fairview Hotel
Grosvenor Hotel
Heron Court
Hilton Hotel
Intercontinental Hotel
Milimani Hotel
New Ainsworth Hotel
New Stanley Hotel
Ngong Hills Hotel
Norfolk Hotel
Panafric Hotel
Safari Park Hotel
Serena Hotel
Sixeighty Hotel
Tropiafric Hotel
Utalii Hotel

Residential Clubs

Mount Kenya Safari Club, Nairobi (Lilian Towers)
Muthaiga Country Club
Nairobi Club
The United Kenya Club

Nairobi National Park

Masai Lodge

Lake Naivasha
Crescent Island Camp
Lake Hotel
Safariland Lodge
Fisherman's Camp (self-help)

Karen
Westwood Park Country Club

Olorgesailie
Self-help *bandas*

Machakos
Machakos Inn

Limuru
Kentmere Club

Golf

18-hole courses
Karen Country Club
Limuru Country Club
Muthaiga Golf Club
Royal Nairobi Golf Club
Sigona Golf Club

9-hole courses
Kiambu Club
Machakos Club
Magadi Golf Club
Naivasha Club
Ndumberi Golf Club
Railway Golf Club
Ruiru Club
Vet. Lab. Golf Club, Kabete

Fishing

Kimakia River—self-help fishing camp
Chania River
Kitamayu River
Thika River
Ruiru Dam
Sasamua Dam

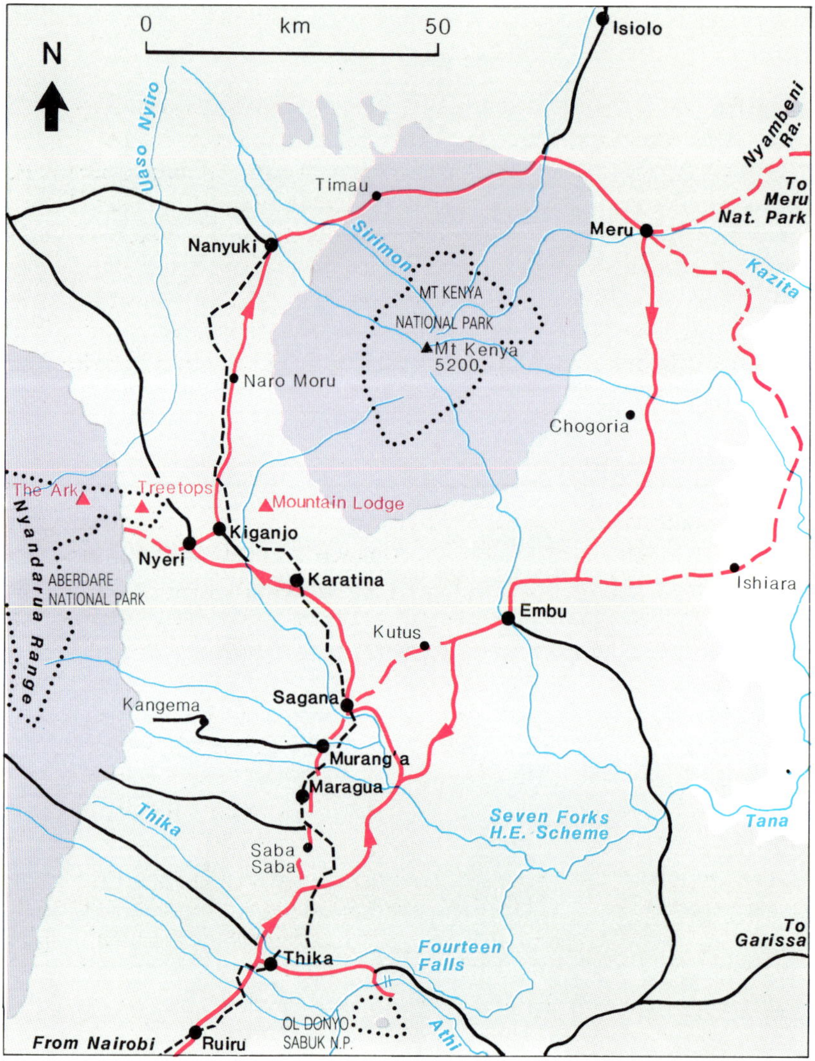

The Mount Kenya region

3 Round Mount Kenya

Three of Kenya's Mountain National Parks lie to the north and north-east of Nairobi—the Aberdare National Park on the Nyandaruas, Ol Donyo Sabuk and Mount Kenya. Nyandarua is a long narrow range running north and south which forms part of the eastern wall of the Rift Valley. Ol Donyo Sabuk is the 2000 metre (7000 feet) high mound a few kilometres south-east of Thika. Mount Kenya, further north on the Equator, has given the country its name. A journey round the mountain takes you along the eastern side of the homeland of the Kikuyu, Kenya's most numerous people—they numbered 3 200 000 in 1979—and back through the country of their ethnic cousins, the Meru and Embu peoples.

Nairobi to Nyeri

Leave the city via Muthaiga and take the 42 km (26 miles) dual carriageway to Thika. The road follows the contour along the base of the Nyandarua foothills, and is quite dull. The Utalii (Tourism) Hotel on your right is where the Government, with Swiss aid, trains hotel staff. At the roundabout after the Benedictine Priory and the Drive-in Cinema are the gates of the General Service Unit, a section of the police force trained to deal with civil disorders, especially big-scale cattle rustling in the dry country. Twin breweries span the Ruaraka River. On the straight stretch beyond them, a Catholic seminary on your right looks across to the Safari Park Hotel and its casino.

A left turn at the next roundabout would take you past Kamiti Prison and up into that part of Kiambu District which grows the world's best coffee. The right turn leads out on to the plains—ranching country, with big patches of black cotton soil, crossed by the Nairobi River and a dozen other streams all draining into the Athi. The flatness is broken by occasional lines of gum trees planted as windbreaks. Your route is straight on, past Kenyatta University College, where most of the country's secondary school teachers qualify.

23 km (14 miles) from Nairobi the road skirts the township of Ruiru. You will notice a small thermal power station to the right of the main road. Its water intake from the river was once blocked when a hippo got stuck across the grille; the animal had eventually to be shot and towed away when bloated. Ruiru High School at the top of the next rise was once the Red Lion Hotel, one of the early European settlers' pubs.

On the right, past the radio station, is Ruiru Sports Club where coffee farmers meet sisal planters of an evening for golf on a pleasant 9-hole layout, just as they did in colonial days when virtually all the players were Europeans. After the next river crossing is the left turn to Gatundu, where Kenya's first President, Mzee Jomo Kenyatta, had his home. More coffee plantation, then a small trading centre called Theririki, with the Jomo Kenyatta College of Agriculture and Technology beyond Juja Police Station to your left and the long low buildings of the East African Bag and Cordage Company to your right. The factory was built in the 1930s by Ake Bursell, who had originally come from Sweden to grow coffee for Karen Blixen at Ngong; later he was the first farmer in the Ruiru area to grow sisal on black cotton soil. The factory turns the local sisal into baler twine and attractive mats. Kalimoni Road on your right leads down to Juja Estate, once the country home of Sir Northrop McMillan, the rich American of vast girth who was knighted for services to Britain in the First World War. He was an experimental farmer on a grand scale, and played host to such visitors as Theodore Roosevelt. He died at sea off Mombasa and is buried on Ol Donyo Sabuk, which was once part of his farm.

After the next crossing of the railway Harries Road on your left leads up to Karamaini, the land which Mr Harries senior decided to buy in 1904. His wife was the first successful grower of smooth-skinned pineapples and is credited with the foundation of the Kenya pineapple industry.

To visit Thika town you leave the main road by the fly-over next to the White Sisters turn-off. Thika claims to be the birthplace of Rugby football in Kenya, back in 1923; it has a number of schools, including the Salvation Army's schools for the blind and Joytown for cripples; its main concern is its industries, notably canning and textiles. The nicest part of Thika is the grounds of the New Blue Posts Hotel, with views of the Chania and Thika falls. To get there you just keep to the main road, ignore the first fly-over and take the second. A left turn here, opposite the Blue Posts, would take you to Kimakia Fishing Camp.

You by-pass Thika township and go out along the Garissa Road in order to visit either Fourteen Falls or Ol Donyo Sabuk. About 19.5 km (12 miles) from Thika you turn right at 'Ol Donyo Sabuk National Park 8 km', then left at the next T-junction. About 2.5 km (1.5 miles) from where you left the Garissa road is a track to the left—no mark or signpost at present—which leads in less than a kilometre to the Athi River and Fourteen Falls. The place where you leave your car can't be seen from the falls, but there is now usually a guard on duty. The Fourteen Falls themselves are never less than pleasant, but after a lot of heavy rain they can be impressive.

For Ol Donyo Sabuk, retrace your steps to the road, cross the Athi, then turn right at the next village. The name means Buffalo Hill in Maasai, and its alternative name, Kilima Mbogo, means the same in Swahili. The National Park itself is quite small—just the upper slopes of the hill. The gazetting of the

Chania Falls, Thika

park in 1969 has probably saved the forest and its birds from extinction. There are still buffalo to be seen in spite of occasional culling. The murram (laterite) tracks are quite passable, but steep in the upper reaches. Sir Northrop McMillan, the owner of the hill earlier in the century, had hoped to be interred at the top when he died, and his hearse was fitted with skis and pulled up by a tractor. However, some of the funeral cars burned out their clutches, so plans were changed and the burial took place on a grassy plateau half-way up. The graves of McMillan, his wife and Louise Decker, the family's nanny, can still be seen. The 360 degree view from the summit is memorable on a clear day.

Returning to the Blue Posts, the dual carriageway ends at the top of the hill as you leave Thika. The crossroads at this point has Thika Sports Club and its 9-hole golf course on your left and the pineapple plantations of Kenya Canners on your right. The Horticultural Research Station further down the road formerly specialized in work on high-altitude sisal. Between here and Mitubiri (Kabati Market) the road crosses papyrus swamps, and you can see on sale papyrus that has been cut and sewn into matting suitable for lining walls or ceilings. After Mitubiri, 13 km (8 miles) from Thika, the road divides at a petrol station. The main road northwards is now straight on to Sagana via Makuyu. The left turn is also a tarmac road of fair quality, but slower. It leads to Sagana via Maragua and Murang'a town.

Choose the left turn if you have time to spare and want to see something of

Murang'a District and the Kikuyu heartland. All this country running from the Nyandarua forest edge down to the plains is divided into parallel east-west ridges by deep valleys which usually have a stream at the bottom. The ridge is so marked a feature of the landscape that the people in the old days adopted it as a social unit.

There were no kings or chiefs in pre-colonial Kikuyuland. Government was carried on through councils of elders at the various levels. The homestead is still the basic unit, but modern farmers' houses are almost all rectangular, even though granny may prefer a traditional round, thatched house in the garden.

The main access roads naturally run up the ridges, and those that carry most traffic nowadays have a tarmac surface. You will see one of them on your left about 4 km (2.5 miles) beyond the trading centre of Saba Saba; it leads up to Kigumo and Kinyona and the territory of old Senior Chief Njiri, who used to welcome guests with his favourite drink of 50 per cent neat gin, 50 per cent neat brandy; Njiri's High School commemorates him.

Probably preferable for getting the flavour of the country in a short time is a second ridge road. You come to it much further on, after passing Maragua Police Station and a large sisal plantation and crossing the Maragua River valley. On your left just as you descend the slope before Murang'a township is the turning to Kahuhia (it has a well-known girls' boarding school and was formerly an Anglican mission station) and Kangema. Note how many of the

Kikuyu-grown maize at Escarpment, with Mount Longonot in background

Coffee with sacks awaiting collection and the factory in the background. Larger estates have their own factories, but in smallholder areas the factory usually belongs to a co-operative. The picked coffee (the 'cherry') is put into a pulper, and the beans which emerge (the 'parchment') are then held in fermentation tanks for three days or so. The beans are then spread out on the drying tables, usually for about fourteen days. It is reckoned that 1,000 kilograms of cherry will yield 200 kilograms of parchement or 160 kilograms of clean coffee when the coffee is heavy.

landholdings that fall away on either side of you are in the form of long narrow strips. This is the result of a farming revolution that took place in the late 1950s, towards the end of the Mau Mau Emergency. The old Kikuyu inheritance system had provided for the division of land between children, and fragmentation had gone to such lengths that many holdings of scattered bits of land were hopelessly uneconomic. Land consolidation to correct this had started in Nyeri back in 1948, and was later introduced in the rest of Kikuyu country. The consolidation committees planned holdings that would produce a good variety of crops and found the new layout satisfactory.

The steeper holdings require terracing, and you will see terraces maintained with varying success. The range of crops naturally changes with the altitude. The main cash crop is coffee in the middle ranges of this country. Lower down it might be tobacco, or pineapples, or even sugar cane. In the higher country, which before Independence was mainly cattle pasture dotted with black wattle, there are now thousands of hectares of tea.

If you persevere up the ridge beyond Kangema you will come to one of the Kenya Tea Development Authority's factories at Kanyenyeini. The right fork in Kanyenyeini itself takes you to a stretch of the South Mathioya River, a trout stream that has a comfortable camp of the private Fly Fishers' Club on its bank; please note that these are not public waters.

A little way beyond and across the river is the trading centre of Tuso, which has one of the earliest Catholic missions established in the highlands, dating from 1902. Karuri, a well-known Murang'a figure at the turn of the century, was in Nairobi for the celebration of King Edward VII's coronation and happened to meet a group of Italian missionaries delayed by unsettled conditions on their way to Ethiopia. He invited them to come and work in his territory, and they accepted the offer. Tuso, now off the beaten track, was in those days on a recognized route of sorts. There was no regular route to the north on the east side of Nyandarua, so the way to get to the Nyeri area, say, from Nairobi was up a track through the Bamboo Forest to the South Kinangop, across the foothills of Nyandarua, then northwards. Tuso was the first centre of habitation that a traveller met on emerging from the forest.

A third ridge road starts in Murang'a township and runs up to Kiriaini, then north to Chinga and Nyeri District. This is the road you start on if you visit the Kikuyu Garden of Eden, *Mukuruweini wa Nyagathanga*. Leave Murang'a on the Kiriaini road, turn left at the trading centre of Kaweru, and then ask for Kabui Primary School; the site with a small museum is close by. The *mukuruwe* is an *albizzia*—a tree with small, almost rectangular leaves whose midribs run from corner to corner. Gikuyu and Mumbi, the local Adam and Eve, lived in this place and had nine daughters, who became the founders of the nine Kikuyu clans.

The township itself has a Martyrs' Church which is worth a visit. The church is an airy, modern building and is decorated with murals by the Tanzanian artist Elimo Njau which illustrate the life of an African Christ. The churchyard has the graves of a number of Christians who were killed during the Emergency, and also that of Francis Hall. Hall came out to work for the Imperial British East Africa Company and later joined the service of the imperial government, first at Kabete, and then here, where he died in 1901. In colonial times Murang'a was known as Fort Hall.

North from Murang'a the road winds down into the valley of the North Mathioya River, then on to Sagana. The river which you cross immediately before Sagana township is the Tana, Kenya's premier river, called here the Sagana. Sagana railway station is of some importance since it is the off-loading point for supplies going to Embu and beyond, and the collecting point for much local produce including tobacco.

For the other quicker route to Sagana, avoiding the detour into Kikuyuland, go straight on at the service station 13 km (8 miles) north of Thika. The road runs through gentle open country with the plantations of Kakuzi Fibrelands on your right running up to the lower slopes of the Ithanga Hills. A left fork would take you to the little trading centre of Makuyu and Punda Milia (Zebra) Estate, where Swift and Rutherfoord pioneered Kenya sisal growing in 1906. Makuyu Club, 4 km (2.5 miles) further on, welcomes visitors to its 9-hole golf course. The road winds through low hills until, at the point where it begins the long descent to the Tana River crossing, there is a superb view of Mount Kenya on a clear day. As you drop down the soil becomes poorer and the inhabitants fewer; the houses are no longer modern and rectangular but old-fashioned and round. As so often in Africa, the river valley, instead of being like the river valleys of Europe fertile and intensively farmed, is the least attractive agricultural proposition in the neighbourhood.

The Tana bridge is the lowest and hottest point on the road. To your left is a small power-station, a poor relative of the sequence of generating stations of the Seven Forks Hydro-Electric Scheme further down stream, which are approached from Thika via the Garissa road. When you have climbed out of the Tana valley you see a right turn leading to Embu. This road runs through the middle of the Mwea/Tebere settlement scheme, where rice is grown under irrigation from the Thiba and Nyamindi Rivers. The original settlers were from Kiambu District, detainees of Mau Mau Emergency days, but they have long since been outnumbered by local settlers from Kirinyaga and Embu. The scheme is Kenya's main local source of rice. In order to visit the Mwea National Reserve you take this Embu road, then turn right again through the village of Karaba and keep going. Beyond the Embu turn-off the soil soon becomes better and the houses more prosperous as you approach Sagana. Rather surprisingly for central Kenya, this is a part of the country where music flourishes; there is usually a primary school choir from this area well-placed in the annual Kenya Music Festival.

Head north out of Sagana on the Nyeri road. Because this is an alluvial plain where the Tana has changed its course many times, the soil is rich. The good crops you see depend on water pumped up from the river and distributed to the many irrigation points on each side of the road.

Beyond the village of Kibirigwi there is a long climb up Pole Pole Hill into the fertile Mathira Division of Nyeri District. Karatina, 128 km (80 miles) from Nairobi, has a flourishing and colourful market on market days, but is otherwise undistinguished.

The first main turning to the left after Karatina is a hard-surface road across the Tana and up to Chinga, another tea-growing area. Next on the right is the fork to Ngandu, the village where Gray Leakey, the late Louis Leakey's cousin, was ritually killed during the Emergency. It now has a respected Catholic girls' secondary school. Immediately afterwards is the left turn to Tumutumu, a Church of Scotland mission founded from Kikuyu in 1908. There is also a girls' secondary school here as well as a hospital. There are three prominent hills in Nyeri District to give you your bearings, and from the top of Tumutumu Hill you can look across to the other two—Karema with its Catholic mission, and

Nyeri Hill with a dome of forest.

6 km (4 miles) beyond Tumutumu the road winds down to the Tana River again. Just before the bridge at Marua there is a turning to the right which is the main road northwards to Kiganjo (Nyeri Station), Naro Moru and Nanyuki. However, go straight on across the river and make the detour of a few kilometres to visit Nyeri, 155 km from Nairobi.

Nyeri is a pleasant town. You enter it past the Catholic Cathedral, a graceful modern building, near which is the turn-off to the Green Hills Hotel. Further up the road is the old White Rhino Hotel started by Sandy Herd, who ran a general store in the town before the First World War. Turn right past the bank and you come to the Central Hotel. The town itself can be dated to 1902, when Richard Meinertzhagen camped here after an expedition against the people of Tetu (a few kilometres up the road westwards) who had massacred an Arab caravan. The site of his camp is supposed to be marked by the trees in the car park of Nyeri Club. An administrative centre was set up shortly afterwards by H.R. Tate. This has now become a fully fledged provincial headquarters, built just beyond the White Rhino and looking across the golf course to the club-house.

Nyeri's main street runs parallel to the road you came in on. It has a post-Uhuru memorial to those Kikuyu who 'Died in the Fight for Freedom 1951–57', and a pre-Uhuru clock-tower in memory of King George V. At the top of the street there is a T-junction where you turn left up an avenue of gums to reach the Outspan Hotel. The Outspan was started by Eric Sherbrooke-Walker and his wife in 1926. It still has most of its old spacious rooms, each complete with a small private verandah by day and a log fire at night, and the garden is a peaceful place. One of the *bandas* down the lawn is Paxtu, where Baden-Powell, the founder of Scouting, spent the last few years of his life from 1938 to 1941.

In the Outspan there is a board giving you the latest state of the roads up on Nyandarua, whether closed, 4-wheel drive only, or open to all cars. A trip up through the cedar forest and bamboo, across the moorland at over 3000 metres (10000 feet), and down the steep drop to the Kinangop and Naivasha is worth making. There is some game, and the waterfalls on the streams on top are pleasing. If you camp in the Aberdare National Park, be warned that the camp sites are high up and can be very cold at night. The National Park has more than one access gate on the eastern side, and the Rohuruini entrance is recommended. You reach it by going up the hill from the Outspan and forking right round the west side of Nyeri Hill. There are adequate signposts.

The Outspan is the base for visits to Treetops Hotel. You see parties from Nairobi having an early lunch in the dining-room before setting off in the afternoon with their armed escort and hostess. They return at breakfast time on the following morning.

The Mountain Park lodges

A few kilometres north of Nyeri is the watershed between the catchment areas of the Tana, draining away to the south, and the Uaso Nyiro, draining to the north. On the southern, wetter side of this watershed, the Nyandarua forest bulges out to the east and the Mount Kenya forest does the same to the west, leaving quite a narrow passage between them. Across this gap in pre-fencing days there used to be regular migrations of elephant from one forest to the other.

The bulge on the Nyandarua side is known as the Treetops Salient, and here are both Treetops itself and also the Ark, a few kilometres to the west. On the Mount Kenya side of the gap is Mountain Lodge, about 20 km (12.5 miles) up towards the mountain from Kiganjo.

All these lodges are built in clearings on the edge of pools and/or salt licks regularly visited by animals. Two of them have bases from which visits are organized, but Mountain Lodge has a car park only a short walk from the entrance. The three lodges all aim at the standard of comfort of a small hotel, with good beds, water on tap and a very respectable cuisine.

Treetops is number one on many people's list. It was the first, having been conceived in the early thirties by Capt. Billy Sheldrick when he and some friends were marooned on a tree platform for several hours by elephant during a

Bongo

safari along the Tana River. He put his idea to Eric Sherbrooke-Walker, who built the first Treetops and opened it in November 1932. The Sheldricks were the first guests. It has been adapted and rebuilt several times since then, notably after Mau Mau burned it down in 1954. It was at Treetops that Queen Elizabeth II was staying when she succeeded to the throne in 1952. The game viewing is good, and large numbers of elephant and buffalo are often seen.

The Ark is a building shaped like the traditional idea of Noah's vessel, and is approached by a wooden bridge over a dry moat. It dates from 1969. It is spacious and comfortable, but viewers may not see the larger herds of game so regularly. On the other hand the rare bongo are not infrequently seen here (a claim which no other lodge can fairly make), and so occasionally are leopard. Its base is the comfortable Aberdare Country Club, a little way off the road from Nyeri to Mweiga. This was formerly the home of Paddy Lyons, a well-known Nyeri farmer. Trout fishing is available from the club for guests.

Mountain Lodge has good and varied game viewing also, usually without either the big battalions or the rarities. Local families often put this lodge first because of the convenience of driving straight there without trans-shipment. Many rooms have their own small balconies looking down on the water-hole. There is a nice roof to walk on, usually with vervet monkeys in attendance.

Nyeri to Nanyuki

Moving on from Nyeri round the mountain, you go back down the avenue from the Outspan to the T-junction at the end, where a detour of a few metres to the right will take you to the Anglican church and to Baden-Powell's grave in the churchyard. However, your road is to the left. Cross the valley of the Chania River, ignore the left turn on the far side which is the road to the Aberdare Country Club, and make for Kiganjo. You pass Nyeri Primary School along Coffee Ridge and then cross the valley of the Tana. 7 km (4.5 miles) from Nyeri you pass the Kenya Police College, the country's main training centre for the force, and rejoin the main Nairobi/Nanyuki road which you left at Marua.

4 km (2.5 miles) beyond Kiganjo is the right turn which leads to Mountain Lodge. The road is adequately marked and takes you past a pleasant small fishing camp on the River Thego and the Sagana State Lodge. This former Royal lodge was a gift from the people of Kenya to Queen Elizabeth II, and was graciously returned to them by Her Majesty at Independence and renamed. From the Thego camp you could also fish the Sagana nearby or the Gura and Chania the other side of Nyeri.

The railway crosses the road as you climb the next hill, then follows a parallel course to the road as far as Naro Moru. The character of the country changes quite suddenly as you reach the watershed. It now becomes wide open grasslands, crossed from time to time by tree-lined river valleys. It is an area of ranches, and was formerly one of the buffer areas marked out by the Protectorate government for European settlement in the first decade of the 20th century. The new settlers were supposed to separate the Kikuyu to the south from the Maasai to the north. Subsequently, in 1911, the Maasai were asked to abandon their northern grazing grounds and use other grazing areas south-west of the Nairobi/Nakuru railway line.

Naro Moru, 177 km (110 miles) from Nairobi, is the familiar cluster of general store, garage, post office and railway station, but more wind-swept than most. Naro Moru River Lodge, 1½ km (1 mile) outside the township, is a pleasant place to stay and is also the most popular base for those wishing to climb Mount Kenya. It has a graded system of accommodation, rising from camp site through climbers' bunk-house to hotel room to self-contained chalet. The lodge can arrange for a porter-guide and porters for you. They have a lot of experience to see that you get from the National Park gate 16 km (10 miles) away up through the forest to the old Meteorological Station (where there are some self-help *bandas*), across the moorland along the Teleki Valley to the scree, round the edge of the Lewis Glacier, up Point Lenana 4968 metres (16 300 feet) and safely down again.

If you have the chance to do a safari up Mount Kenya, take it. It is worth the effort. But be careful. Most of the tracks through the forest are also game trails. Also, there is a risk of pulmonary oedema at high altitudes, so spend several days on the ascent if you can, to avoid the danger of altitude sickness if you climb too fast. Take proper clothes and boots and equipment. If you want to climb the peak, consult first the Mountain Club of Kenya, PO Box 45741, Nairobi.

Many routes up Mount Kenya have been found since Sir Halford Mackinder first climbed Batian in 1899. In earlier days most people went up from Chogoria, on the east side. Nowadays the track from the Naro Moru gate to the Met. Station is the most used. To go up to the moorland by car the Sirimon Track is recommended. It is on the northern slopes of the mountain, beyond Nanyuki. It follows the course of the Sirimon River, and the upper forest reaches are particularly beautiful when the mumondos (*hagenia*)—the trees which grow highest on the mountain—are in full pink flower.

The 23 km (14 miles) from Naro Moru to Nanyuki are still mainly ranching country. There are some fine cedar and wild olive trees in the patch of forest where you cross the Burguret River. From Bantu Utamaduni Lodge to the right you can fish for trout. Arnold Paice, the first European settler in the district, arrived in 1910 and lived on the banks of the last stream before the township. He raised pigs, and sent them on the hoof all the way to Uplands Bacon Factory.

You cross the Equator as you enter the town. In fact it runs through the middle of the New Silverbeck Hotel on your right. Nanyuki is quite a

Smallholdings between Nyeri and Embu

substantial place, being the railhead for a large farming area and also an army garrison town. There is a club with a 9-hole golf course. A second hotel, the Sportsman's Arms, is close by. A short distance out of town to the south-east is the Mount Kenya Safari Club, expensive and well run, one of the most comfortable places to stay in the whole country. It started life as a private house, became the Mawingo (Clouds) Hotel after the Second World War, and was converted into a club in 1958 by a distinguished syndicate that included the late William Holden. It offers daily membership to visitors on weekdays. To get there you can take Kenyatta Drive to the right after the Silverbeck.

North of the Mountain

The left turn at the end of Nanyuki's main street would take you to the Uaso Nyiro River and Laikipia. Your route is straight on past the Catholic church and out of town on the Isiolo and Meru road. The first main turning to the left leads to the Loldaiga Hills. In the hills, which are rocky and not blest with ample rain, the late Douglas Hinde over more than 40 years turned his 16 000 hectares (40 000 acres) into an outstanding ranch that now has many miles of piping and scores of water points and small dams to put whatever rain falls to good use.

14 km (9 miles) out of Nanyuki is the Sirimon River, and the Sirimon Track

up the mountain starts at a turning to the right just before the valley crossing. It is properly marked. In Timau, 22 km (nearly 14 miles) from Nanyuki, the signpost on your right reads 'Kentrout', and this is worth the detour of 3 km (2 miles) up a dirt road if you need lunch. Kentrout is a commercial trout hatchery which has an open-air restaurant that serves the fish grilled on charcoal.

Your road beyond Timau goes over the shoulder of the mountain up through wheat and sheep land to above 2590 metres (8500 feet). On a clear day the views to your left over the hot country are spectacular; you may be able to make out the beginning of the Mathews Range to the north; the Nyambenis are closer to your far right. Near the highest point of the road a farm sign on your left reads '*Kisima*', i.e. Spring. This farm dates from the 1919 Soldier Settlement Scheme, when it was drawn in the lottery by Will Powys, the farmer brother of a Somerset literary family that included Llewellyn, T.F. and J.C. Powys. Will became a highly successful sheep breeder after some early disasters—he once bought 1200 sheep in 1925 from Somalis, brought them up to Kisima, and lost over 200 of them dead after their first night in the cold mist and rain. He died in 1976, but his family still farms in Kenya.

You have been in Meru District since soon after leaving Nanyuki, but shortly after Kisima the road drops sharply into old-established Meru farmland. The Kibirichia area grows good potatoes. At the foot of the hill the left turning leads to Isiolo and the Samburu and Buffalo Springs National Reserves (see Chapter 8). It is also the way you go by land to Addis Ababa or Mogadishu. Your road ahead leads through some farming land and a short stretch of forest to Meru township, 12 km (7.5 miles) further on.

Meru and Embu

Meru is a busy commercial centre for an area that produces a lot of good coffee and tea. The people used to have a form of indigenous parliament, and this still survives despite public affairs being now run by the provincial administration. Accommodation and food are available at the Pig and Whistle and Meru County Hotels. There is fishing in the Mutonga, the Kazita and other streams. The club used to have a 9-hole golf course on the grassy triangle of land behind the District Headquarters, but this, alas, has not been kept up. The Kazita River runs through the lower part of the town and provides its water supply. There is a Meru Museum that shows you how life was traditionally lived. The town is also a church centre. The Italian mission effort started from Mathari, outside Nyeri, and spread from there round the mountain and north to the Ethiopian border. Meru is now the seat of a Catholic bishop. The Methodist Church also has a centre on the northern outskirts of the town at Kaaga, where the educational institutions include a girls' secondary school and a teachers' college.

To visit Meru Game Park you go back out of town by the way you came in and turn right where this is signposted. The road passes through Kaaga, and the teachers' college on your left is worth visiting if you can get permission. (It is now a Government college and no longer run by the Methodist Church.) The forest trees in the grounds are particularly good, and the college's main sports field was the parade ground of the King's African Rifles in the days when a battalion was stationed here to look after law and order in the old Northern Frontier District.

It is a long 80 km (50 miles) from Meru to the edge of the park, and the road used to be an ordeal when much of the surface was rough and stony—dust in dry weather and mud in the rains. It now has a good tarmac surface to the Maua turn-off. You go out across the neck of lower land between Mount Kenya and the Nyambeni Range, through Kianjai and Karama, cross the Nyambenis at Ithanga, then, leaving Maua and its Methodist mission hospital on your right, make the long descent from 1800 metres (6000 feet) to 600 metres (2000 feet). This last stretch is a dirt road usually in fair condition, and the tracks inside the park itself are well maintained. The prosperity of the Nyambeni foothills depends on the growing of *miraa*, a bush whose twigs are chewed to produce a mild narcotic. Large amounts of *miraa* are consumed in northern Kenya, Somalia, and even across in South Yemen, where the plant is known as *khat*.

You enter Meru National Park by the Murera Gate and the Meru Mulika Lodge, the chief place to stay, is 6 km (4 miles) further on. Not much further and to the left, duly signposted, is Leopard Rock Lodge, one of the better equipped self-help lodges in the Kenya game parks, with a good site on the Murera River. It is operated by Meru County Council. There is also a group of camp sites and some more self-help *bandas* near the park headquarters, bookable through the Warden and the Parks Administration. A number of special camp-sites, particularly along the Rojeweru and other streams, are available for those with their own equipment, but these must be booked in advance through the National Parks organization. 'Pippa's Camp' down towards the Kenmare Ford is not one of them—its name recalls the work of Joy Adamson with cheetahs (*The Spotted Sphinx*). The Adamsons had much to do with the early history of the Meru Park, though George Adamson has now moved across the Tana River and is busy helping to establish on the south bank the Kora Game Reserve, gazetted in 1976.

Meru Park is an attractive place with plenty of game, including a few white rhinos, not to be seen elsewhere in Kenya, good birds, and, because it is low, hot and well-watered, masses of insect life. Put up with the mosquitoes and miscellaneous beetles at night, and enjoy the antics of the dung beetles by day. A trip along the Tana during your stay is worth doing, since the river down here is impressive. In dry weather, if you are returning to Nairobi via Embu, you can leave the park by the Ura Gate in the south-west corner and drive across the plains, keeping the Nyambenis on your right, to a junction with the Embu-Meru low road.

The southern slopes of the Nyambenis must have a claim to be the wettest part of Kenya. 3800 mm (150 inches) of rain in a year have been recorded. As you would expect, it is a tea-growing area. The districts of Igembi and Tigania on the drier plains below, between you and the hills, are by tradition the early home of the Mount Kenya peoples, including the Kikuyu, from which they began their migration to the south and east, probably in the 15th century. They appear to have supplanted or absorbed the hunting peoples who occupied the area before them, the Gumba and the Dorobo.

At one time it was thought that all the Mount Kenya peoples had reached their present homes from the coast, having retreated up the Tana River in the face of Galla invasion from the north. More recent research shows this to be unlikely. But the Meru do have this tradition of having migrated to their present home from somewhere to the east known as *Mbwa*, which may possibly have been Manda Island, near Lamu. However, the migration of the Meru people was a later event. They probably did not reach Tharakaland in the Meru low country before the first half of the 18th century.

Continuing the circuit of the mountain from Meru township, you have a choice of routes. After crossing the Kazita River out of town past the Pig and Whistle, you can turn left down the hill and cover a wide arc out across the plains which eventually brings you back up again into Embu via Ishiara. This is a murram road, usually in fair shape, pleasant but unexciting. The alternative route is the 137 km (85 miles) of road much nearer to the mountain which pass through Chogoria, winding in and out of the valleys. Tarmac is being laid on it at the time of writing.

There are some points of interest on this second route if you can ever afford to take you eyes off the road. Notice what a lot of indigenous trees there are on the hillsides of the farms in the Meru areas; this is because there is a rule among the Meru people—rare in this part of the world—that trees felled must be replaced by fresh planting. Nkubu has a hospital and a secondary school. At Egoji there is a girls' secondary school and a big college for teachers. Chogoria is a market centre and has a hospital. The Church of Scotland mission station here, up towards Mount Kenya, was founded from Kikuyu in 1908; for many years it has been associated with the Irvine family. The track up the mountain from here leads to self-help *bandas* on the moorland built by Meru County Council. The country which you pass through until you reach Chuka township is part of the area that the Chuka Drummers come from, a famous ensemble who often perform in Nairobi on national occasions. The dialect spoken here is much closer to the Kikuyu language than to either the Meru tongue spoken to the north or the Embu one to the south, the reason being no doubt that this was

Mount Kenya: the Teleki Valley, with giant groundsel and giant lobelia

along the route of the migration from Tigania/Igembe and was where a sizeable group related to those who later pushed on to Murang'a decided to break off and settle down.

Embu town is now the headquarters of the Eastern Province. It is a pleasant well-treed place built on a gently sloping hillside between two rivers, the Kapingazi to the north and the Rupingazi to the south. At the top end of the town is Kangaru High School, and below it the Izaak Walton Inn, a popular centre for trout fishing. There is a furrow running parallel with the main street on its north side and several of the houses here have beautiful gardens, thanks to plentiful water. There was at one time a 9-hole golf course laid out by a former proprietor of the inn, but the council decided around the time of Independence to plough it up for agricultural purposes. Later, when it was found that the extra maize and beans brought less profit to the town than its past golfing visitors, the township fathers asked the proprietor if he would put the golf course back again, but he declined. However, the fishing is still reported to be good.

From Embu the Nairobi road is to the south-west. You can if you wish turn right at Samson's Corner, 11 km (7 miles) out of town, and drive via Kutus, where you turn right towards the mountain for the Thiba Fishing Camp, due north of Kianyaga. Beyond Kutus is Kaggio, and then the Nairobi/Nyeri T-junction at Sagana.

The main road to the city goes straight on at Samson's Corner and passes through the Mwea/Tebere rice scheme. If you come this way the take-off point where water is led from the Nyamindi to the rice-fields is a nice stretch of highland river; there is a track to it from the village of Kimbimbi. When you rejoin the Nyeri/Nairobi road north of the Tana bridge you have completed your circuit of the mountain.

Places to stay

Ruaraka
Safari Park Hotel

Thika
New Blue Posts Hotel

Nyeri
Outspan Hotel
Green Hills Hotel
Central Hills Hotel
White Rhino Hotel
Nyeri Inn

Mweiga
Treetops
The Ark
Aberdare Country Club

Kiganjo
Mountain Lodge

Naro Moru
Naro Moru River Lodge
Bantu Utamaduni Lodge
Self-help *bandas* at the Meteorological Station

Nanyuki
Mount Kenya Safari Club
Sportsman's Arms
New Silverbeck Hotel

Isiolo
Wilderness Trails

Meru
Pig and Whistle Hotel
Meru County Hotel

Meru National Park
Meru Mulika Lodge
Leopard Rock Safari Lodge (self-help)
National Park *bandas* (self-help, at camp site 3 km (2 miles) from park headquarters)

Chogoria
Self-help *bandas* up on the moorland

Embu
Izaak Walton Inn

Mountain climbing and walking

Facilities at Naro Moru River Lodge
Consult the Mountain Club of Kenya, PO Box 45741, Nairobi

Golf

9-hole courses

Ruiru Sports Club
Thika Sports Club
Makuyu Club
Nyeri Club
Nanyuki Club
Mount Kenya Safari Club

Fishing

Southern Nyandaruas

Kimakia River (fishing camp—self-help)
Chania River (Thika)

Eastern Nyandaruas

Gura River
Chania River (Nyeri)
Amboni River (Aberdare Country Club—full services)

Note Kiandongoro Fishing Lodge (self-help) up on the moorland on the Magura River in the Aberdare National Park: address—c/o Mountain National Parks, PO Box 24, Mweiga.

North-eastern Nyandaruas

Ngobit River

Western Mount Kenya

Naro Moru River (Naro Moru River Lodge—full services)

North-eastern Mount Kenya

Kazita River
Mutonga River

Southern Mount Kenya

Thego River (fishing camp—self-help)
Sagana River
Thiba River (fishing camp—self-help)
Nyamindi River
Karinga River
Rupingazi River (Izaak Walton Inn—full services)

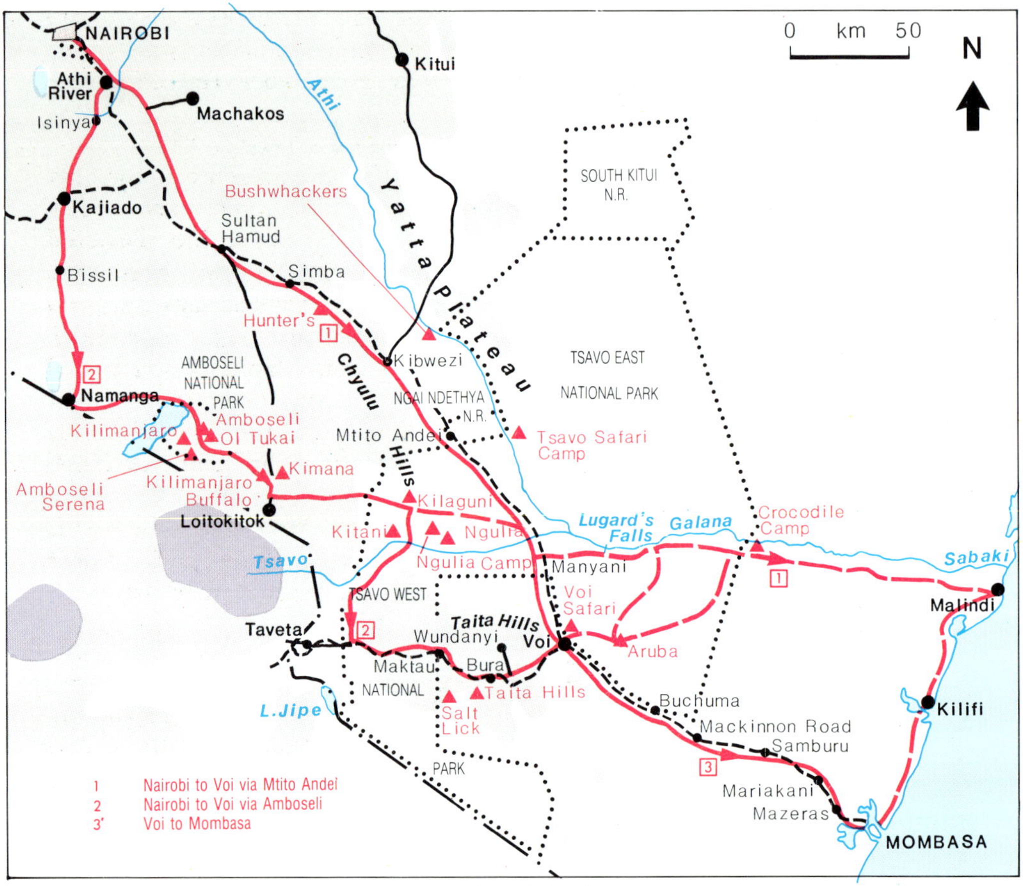

Nairobi to Mombasa

4 Nairobi to Mombasa

Nairobi to Mombasa is nowadays an easy journey. Several buses make the trip daily and nightly, the air service is quick and convenient, and the train, by far the nicest way to go, still makes its stately 13-hour progress between the old and the new capitals.

While Mombasa was the chief town of the British East Africa Protectorate, from 1895 to 1907, the railway took over from the caravan route as the only practicable means of getting up-country. However, when motor-cars became common and roads were made, the route between Nairobi and Mombasa did not follow the railway line. Instead it started out from Nairobi towards the south end of the Ngong Hills, turned left to Kajiado, and went all the way round via Kilimanjaro to the coast. The present direct route dates only from 1926, when it was pioneered by Galton Fenzi, a Kiambu coffee farmer who founded the local Automobile Association, and Captain Gethin. They had to make various stretches of the route as they went along. The old Riley in which they did it, registration B3, is still in running order and kept at the Jacaranda Hotel in Westlands.

In this chapter we follow two alternative routes to Mombasa. The first is down the main road. The second, which visits the southern game parks, makes a loop more like the original road route between Nairobi and the coast.

Nairobi to Voi via Mtito Andei

Leave town by the Uhuru Highway to the south-east out past Jomo Kenyatta Airport. At Embakasi Station you leave Nairobi and enter the Machakos District of Eastern Province. As you descend the slope to Athi River, 27 km (17 miles) from Nairobi, the Kenchic Poultry Hatchery is on your left and the eastern tip of Nairobi Game Park on your right with the local cement factory beyond. Leave on your right the turning to Kajiado and the Tanzanian border, cross the Athi River and proceed past the Kenya Meat Commission's factory. *Athi*, you may recall, is the Kikuyu word for hunters. It is used by them to refer to some of the Wandorobo or hunting/gathering peoples who previously lived in the present Kikuyuland.

From now on the country becomes gradually drier, the trees fewer, and the grass browner and even almost grey between the rains. These wide open spaces are of limited scenic interest, but the broad view is never entirely featureless between Nairobi and Mombasa, since there are always hills, or even a mountain, to be seen somewhere in the landscape.

9 km (6 miles) after the Meat Commission is the Small World Country Club. The farmers on the ranch to the south of it have been experimentally running game for years, on the theory that people like venison as well as beef, and buck may be more efficient than cattle at turning grass into meat without causing erosion. The jagged-edged hill on your left 1 km (0.6 mile) beyond is Lukenya, where the Mountain Club of Kenya has a good camp site. The faces of Lukenya contain examples in miniature of many of the technical difficulties of rock-climbing, so it is a popular practice ground.

The turn-off to Machakos is 46 km (28 miles) from Nairobi. The high ground on your left before the turning is the south end of the Mua Hills, an area where fruit will grow and where Kenya Orchards has its factory for jams and marmalades. President Theodore Roosevelt stayed up in these hills with Sir Alfred Pease when he came on a safari arranged by the hunter F. C. Selous in 1909. He was interested in going after lion on the Kapiti Plains to your right.

For the next 50 km (30 miles) or so the road runs through a salient of former European farming land, the southern tip of the old White Highlands. The railway is the dividing line between Maasai country to the south and Kamba country to the north. To reduce raiding and general friction along such boundaries the colonial government early in the century followed a policy of creating buffer areas and inviting white settlers to live and farm in them.

Several of the European families of Machakos and Ulu along this road farmed continuously throughout most of the colonial period, from the early days of ostrich farming onwards. Over the years they raised the carrying capacity of their ranches by rotational grazing, building dams and sinking boreholes. Nearest to Nairobi were the Percivals, on whose land the gates, as you will see, are still marked Potha Estate; then came the Hills. Further down the road, where it rises at 80 km (50 miles) from Nairobi to cross the Ulu hills, are the Joyce (with airstrip) and Wilson farms. The late Major Frank Joyce, CBE, in addition to running this farm, Kilima Kiu, for nearly half a century, was one of the Europeans who worked hard for the development of African land and was honoured by the Wakamba for doing so. He died in 1959, but at the time of writing the farm is still in the family.

As you drop down from Ulu a road to the left leads to the Kilungu Hills, one of the pleasant oases of Ukambani. Next, a secondary road right leads to Kiu Station and on to Selengei, where there is a good place to camp. Near it the Maasai in the dry season dig pits in the bed of the sand river to reach water for their cattle. 5 km (3 miles) further on is the turning to Kima Station, where during the construction of the railway Inspector Ryall was dragged out of his carriage by a lion. He is buried in the cemetery next to the Railway golf course in Nairobi.

There is usually some game between here and the small trading centre of Sultan Hamud, said to be named after an Arab visitor of the 1890s. The turn-off through Sultan Hamud, or later after crossing the railway line at Emali, takes you on to the pipeline road leading to the Amboseli National Park and Loitokitok.

The next point of interest is Simba, where there are springs of fresh water and tanks have been made for watering Maasai cattle. About 160 km (100 miles) from Nairobi you cross the Kiboko River and see immediately on your right the small hotel called Hunter's Lodge. This is worth a visit, if only to look at its well-treed garden on the river and plentiful birds while drinking something cool. The lodge is named, by the way, after a professional hunter whose surname happened to be Hunter and who had a favourite camp site here.

Continue past Makindu with its striking Sikh temple, originally built by Indian engineers working on the railway at the turn of the century. Trees increase as you near Kibwezi and you pass through the edge of the Kibwezi Forest. At one point the road crosses quite a broad lava flow, reminding you that the Chyulu Hills to the south are a legacy of recent volcanic activity. Kibwezi itself is by-passed by the main road, and it has little of interest these days. In 1891 the East African Industrial Mission opened its only station here, but it made no great mark; in 1898 the Rev. Thomas Watson moved the mission lock, stock and barrel to Kikuyu, near Nairobi, where it became famous under Church of Scotland direction.

If you take the left turn from Kibwezi towards Kitui you will see a sign on your right after about 16 km (10 miles) indicating the route to what most people call Bushwhackers, though its official name is Masalani Camp. It is a fine site on the banks of the Athi River where Hugh Stanton, a game trapper, used to house his animals prior to shipment abroad. There is still a peaceful self-help camp here. The birds are good and the river interesting, especially when in spate. After the Bushwhackers turning, the road from Kibwezi crosses the Athi and then climbs over the Yatta Plateau; it continues, rather rough and crossed by many dry stream-beds, via the small plant reserve at Mutomo to Kitui.

Bushwhackers used to be quite isolated and surrounded by game, like an extension of the Tsavo East National Park whose western tip is a short distance downstream. But now all the big game has gone and there are patches of cultivation. This is all part of a substantial expansion to the south-east on the part of the Kamba people in recent years.

The main road continues with the long chain of the Chyulu Hills on the right; the parallel ridge on your left, on the far side of the Athi River, is the Yatta Plateau, a single very long lava flow which forms your north-easterly horizon for kilometres. 236 km (146 miles) from Nairobi you reach Mtito Andei, roughly half-way to the coast. The Tsavo Inn is here if you want to break your journey. There is also an Automobile Association post just by the Caltex filling

Klipspringer

station. A track by the Total station leads across the railway line to Tsavo Safari Camp, just across the Athi River. On the opposite side of the road to the Tsavo Inn is the main entrance to Tsavo West National Park.

Tsavo is by far the largest of Kenya's National Parks and is famous for its elephants. It is divided by the main road into two sections, Tsavo East and Tsavo West, each under its own warden. Tsavo East is the flatter area, at least in the part open to the public, but it has a most interesting stretch of the Athi River, here called the Galana. (The river starts as the Athi, becomes the Galana in its middle reaches, and flows into the sea as the Sabaki.) All that part of the park which is north of the river is closed to the public. Tsavo West has interesting scenery with the Ngulia range of hills, the tip of the Chyulus, Chiemu Crater with its klipspringer, the hill called Poacher's Lookout, lava flows and Mzima Springs. It extends south to the Tanzanian border.

The whole of Tsavo Park has suffered badly from poaching. Back in the 1950s and 1960s this scourge was worrying, but it was contained. The insatiable demand for ivory and rhino horn (much valued in the Far East for imagined medicinal and aphrodisiac properties, and in Arabia for dagger handles) led to attempts by businessmen in Mombasa to provide the supply. Their method was to send agents to induce the Waliangulu, hunters and gatherers who live along the inner fringe of the coastal strip, to step up their hunting, brew more arrow poison, and produce a surplus for export.

These plans were eventually defeated by the National Parks staff, with the help of the local officers of the Game Department. Some of the best poachers were skilfully turned and became equally effective gamekeepers. There were successful prosecutions of dealers in the Mombasa courts, and poaching was greatly reduced.

During the 1970s poaching staged a revival. This time the dealers did not rely on local hunters armed with bows and arrows. Instead they employed Somalis who lived away from the park area and only entered it to stage quick raids armed with modern automatic weapons. Nowadays the Government anti-poaching unit based out at Ngong has again brought this crime under control. But the game board in Taita Hills Lodge last time I saw it nevertheless read 'Rhino—believed extinct in area due to poaching'.

Despite these losses there is still a lot of game to be seen; moreover Tsavo has a certain grandeur and should not be missed. Besides the elephants there are buffalo, lion and cheetah, and a wide range of plains game; but the landscape seems to stay in people's memories as firmly as the animals. In Tsavo West there are two fully-equipped lodges, Kilaguni facing the Chyulus and Ngulia, on a hilltop overlooking the Tsavo River valley, as well as two self-help lodges; one is at Kitani, south-west of Kilaguni, and the other, Ngulia Safari Camp, a few kilometres from the lodge of that name. There is a pleasant camping site just inside the Mtito Andei park entrance; but if the grass is long, look out for

Tsavo elephants

pepper ticks with which I was once infested here. If you are not familiar with these little horrors, they are best taken off the skin one by one with the help of paraffin.

To go by way of Tsavo West makes a very pleasant detour on the way from Nairobi to the coast, especially if you have the time to make an overnight stop. Enter the park at Mtito Andei, not forgetting to buy your map. Plan a route that will allow you to visit Mzima Springs, two-thirds of the way from Kilaguni to Kitani, where an abundant flow of water, coming under ground from the Chyulu Hills, creates an oasis and deep pools with hippo and crocodile; there is a nature trail and an observation cabin from which you can see the hippos moving under water. Mzima Springs is at present a large part of Mombasa's water supply. You leave the park by the Tsavo Gate in order to rejoin the main road. The circular track to the Tsavo Gate along the banks of the Tsavo River is the nicest route, but nowadays this is recommended for 4-wheel drive vehicles only. There is a camp site by the river about 1 km (0.6 miles) inside the Tsavo Gate.

If you are not making a detour through Tsavo West, continue down the main road from Mtito Andei. There are sometimes elephants to be seen along this stretch, and on your left, on a parallel course with yours, are the railway, then the Galana River, and the Yatta Plateau beyond. The next significant landmark is the bridge over the Tsavo River, 284 km (175 miles) from Nairobi. It was here in 1898 that two man-eating lions terrorized the camps of the Indian labourers working on the construction of the railway, carrying off more than two dozen victims over a period of nine months. At one time there was a mass exodus of labour back to the coast and work was held up for three weeks. But eventually the lions were shot by the engineer sent out to build the Tsavo railway bridge, Lt-Col J. H. Patterson, who wrote an account of the episode called *The Man Eaters of Tsavo*. A few years later Patterson served from 1907 to 1909 as Kenya's first Game Warden.

296 km (185 miles) from Nairobi you reach Manyani. On your left is the Manyani Gate into Tsavo East National Park, and then on your right a prison. From here it is a straight run of 19 km (12 miles) past the Taita Hills on your right to Voi and its sisal plantations. After you cross the railway line coming in from Taveta and the Tanzanian border there is a crossroads. A right turn would take you to the Taita Hills and Salt Lick Lodges, left into Voi township, while the main Mombasa road is straight on. You go through the township to reach the Voi Gate, the main entrance into Tsavo East.

If you decide to break your journey to the coast by an overnight stop in Tsavo East National Park, there are two lodges to stay at: Voi Safari Lodge, which has full facilities, and the self-help lodge at Aruba on the edge of Aruba Dam. There is also a camping site just inside the main Voi Gate. However, it is better to enter the park by the Manyani Gate. Once inside, the road southwards will

The Taita Hills

take you on a course parallel with the railway to Mudanda Rock, a large whale-backed outcrop overlooking a pool; there is a natural ledge on the eastern side from which you can look down on elephants watering at the pool. Continuing south past the rock you come to Voi Safari Lodge 5 km (3 miles) short of the township. Be careful, by the way, to reach any of these National Park entrance gates before 5 p.m.; if you arrive later you will be very unpopular.

For a longer and more interesting route proceed eastwards inside the Manyani Gate and follow the course of the Galana River. After about 13 km (8 miles) you will reach a point where the river narrows and then virtually disappears into a rocky gorge, to re-appear in a series of rapids over the rocks. These are the Lugard Falls, visited by Lugard in 1890 on his way to take over the administration of Uganda for the Imperial British East Africa Company. Continue following the course of the river, along which the game normally collects in the dry season, keeping a sharp look-out for lesser kudu, a fine antelope with spiral horns and striped white coat. Then turn right at the point called Sobo to Aruba Lodge.

Wherever you stop, whether at Voi Lodge or Aruba, you can continue through the park to another exit gate. A comparatively short drive in a south-easterly direction will take you to the Buchuma Gate at the southern end of the park out on to the Mombasa road. Alternatively you can follow the track east and then north towards the river and leave the park at the Sala Gate; this is a more direct though more lonely route if you are heading for Malindi and wish to by-pass Mombasa. Just after you leave the park on this road there is a turning to the left which takes you to Crocodile Tented Lodge, a comfortable place on the south bank of the river, now called the Sabaki from here to the sea. The distance from the lodge to Malindi is 100 km (62 miles).

Nairobi to Voi via Amboseli

For this route turn to the right on to the Kajiado/Namanga road just before Athi River, 27 km (17 miles) from Nairobi. Go south past the Athi River Gate to Nairobi National Park and the cement factory and up past Athi River Prison. You are now in Maasai country. These are broad open grasslands, sometimes stony, with few big trees and a lot of small streams, many of them only seasonal. To your right are the Athi Plains and the game conservation area called Kitengela. To the left the plains are called Kapiti, a corruption of Kaputei, which is the name of the section of Maasai who live there.

About 30 km (19 miles) from Athi River you reach Isinya, where the only prominent feature is the Rural Training Centre on your left. In 1961 the NCCK (National Christian Council of Kenya), with Church Missionary Society aid, took over this former detention camp to start a centre, the purpose being to help the local Maasai recover from the disastrous drought and floods of 1960–1 and to promote Maasai development in general. There is a primary school, a church, a tannery and a village polytechnic. Village polytechnics were pioneered by NCCK and are now a feature of Kenyan rural life; they offer trade training and practical skills to those who have missed secondary school places. The Handicrafts Centre, which brings in some money by selling ornaments and beadwork to tourists, was started as an afterthought to give the girls some useful employment.

Isinya has proved popular and other such centres have been opened in Maasailand, usually starting as 'ranch aid stores' to sell things like insecticides for cattle dips, then adding other facilities.

Kajiado itself is reached 51 km (31 miles) from Athi River, 78 km (46 miles) from Nairobi. It is the southern of the two administrative centres for Kenya Maasailand, the northern one being Narok. The railway station is on the branch line that carries soda ash from Magadi to the main line at Konza. The township has an African Inland church, a mosque, schools and the district hospital.

South of Kajiado the road crosses hilly country with more bush and flat-topped thorns. There is still game to be seen, and the country is pleasant without being spectacular. Occasionally you see a Maasai homestead, or *enkang*, surrounded by its thorn fence. 29 km (18 miles) after Kajiado you pass

Bissil, a small trading centre. As you near Namanga, the Kenya border township, vegetation becomes richer and there is some forest. About 58 km (36 miles) from Bissil you will see the entrance to Namanga River Hotel, lying at the foot of Ol Donyo Orok, the Black Hill, 2526 metres (8290 feet) high.

The road between the hotel and the border post is lined with sellers of Maasai curios and ornaments, and usually there are some ochred *moran* (warriors) standing about holding their spears. They used to allow their photographs to be taken for a substantial fee, but this is now officially forbidden; please do not photograph the Maasai. The *moran* used of course to fulfil an important role in their society, but nowadays they have little to do. Nor do they have wives to think of, since by Maasai custom the warrior age-set is not allowed to marry.

The turning to Amboseli is on your left before the border post. But before you reach the park entrance and Lake Amboseli there is a long drive on a dirt road, much of it corrugated as a result of many years of drivers ignoring the speed limit. However, there is game to be seen, notably the long-necked gerenuk, who seem to like this thorn bush, and once you are beyond the first ridges there can be good distant views of Amboseli itself and Kilimanjaro. The distance from Namanga to Ol Tukai is some 72 km (45 miles); you reach the edge of Lake Amboseli about three-quarters of the way there.

'Lake' is a misnomer for most of the year, since this is a broad salt pan that can be crossed in a car during the dry season. Keep to the car tracks to avoid

Sunset at Amboseli

getting bogged down in a damp patch. If in doubt, keep to the slightly longer main track round the lake edge.

There has been a long history of debate between the Government and the Maasai over the relative claims of wildlife and cattle on the grazing and water in this area. The amicable upshot has been that within the fairly extensive game reserve, shared by wild animals and pastoralists, there is a small National Park for the animals only; but the Maasai have been compensated for the lost land by the sinking of boreholes for their cattle elsewhere.

This really is a small park, and it tends to get quite crowded, especially at weekends, being relatively close to Nairobi. It is a favourite with many people, partly because there is so much game to see just round the swamp, even if the more famous rhinos have now been poached, and partly because Kilimanjaro makes such a splendid backdrop. In the central area are Amboseli Lodge, Kilimanjaro Safari Lodge and a self-help lodge called Ol Tukai which is the oldest accommodation here for visitors.

Amboseli Serena Lodge is a little way south, and the camp sites are now west of the swamp. Kilimanjaro Buffalo Lodge is to the south-east, in the vicinity of the Kimana Gate.

Leave Amboseli by the road from Ol Tukai south-east to the Kimana Gate through 35 km (22 miles) of open country. Turn right and then left a few kilometres later to cross the Emali–Loitokitok pipeline road and get on to the

Amboseli rhino

link road leading into Tsavo West National Park. If you continued down the pipeline road you would find at Loitokitok the Kenya Outward Bound Training School.

The road into Tsavo crosses a plain between Kilimanjaro on your right and the Chyulu Hills on your left until 83 km (51 miles) from Ol Tukai you reach the park boundary. The Chyulu Gate, however, is still some distance ahead, on the far side of the big Shaitani lava flow. *Shaitani*, meaning Devil, is the volcanic cone away to your left; it has a vaguely evil local reputation. Not far inside the gate is Kilaguni Lodge.

As we have noted, there are four main places to stay in Tsavo West, Kilaguni itself, Ngulia Lodge, Ngulia Safari Camp, and Kitani Self-Help Lodge. If you are going to follow the southerly route out of the park after a night stop, it is best to stay either at Kilaguni or at Kitani. Proceed south from Kilaguni on the Kitani road, making a detour to Mzima Springs if you have not seen them. Follow the signposts to the Mbuyuni Gate, 62 km (39 miles) beyond Kitani to the south. At Mbuyuni you emerge on to the main road leading from the Tanzanian border through Taveta to Voi.

If you turn right it is only a short distance to Taveta, an oasis lying between Lake Chala to the north and Lake Jipe to the south. The people of Taveta are closely related to the Wataita of the Taita Hills. It was at Taveta that Colonel Ewart Grogan, founder of Gertrude's Garden Children's Hospital in Nairobi, lived towards the end of his life, building himself a spacious farmhouse. He experimented with various crops and produced some excellent oranges, but finally settled for growing sisal. Grogan is the only man known to have walked from the Cape to Cairo, a feat which he did as a young man apparently in order to convince his future father-in-law that he had done something. It was also at Taveta during the First World War that the German forces made an early incursion into British territory in 1914; the British garrison, consisting of Hugh Lafontaine and five tribal police, carried out a fighting withdrawal.

South of Mbuyuni there is a further vast stretch of the Tsavo West park, and a drive through it to the shores of Lake Jipe is worth doing if you are interested in birds; the bird life round the lake has a great variety, and not only of water birds. Ask at the Mbuyuni Gate for directions on how to get there. There is no lodge at the lake, but there is a large open *banda* with a thatched roof and no walls; inside it are two little rooms with walls where you can sleep if you wish. The set-up is very much self-help. The Kenya/Tanzania border runs down the middle of the lake, and there is a fine view across the water to Tanzania's Pare Mountains.

Return to the main road and turn east. Once you reach Maktau, where there is another Tsavo West gate, you are outside the park territory and have covered half the 114 km (71 miles) between Taveta and Voi. Another 17 km (10.5 miles) brings you in sight of Taita Hills Lodge to your right. There is a pair of well-

Krapf's church, as rebuilt in 1879

equipped lodges here, Taita Hills and Salt Lick, and they are run in tandem; if you have booked in to Salt Lick, but arrive in time for lunch, it is served to you at Taita Hills. This is a building in the style of a German fort, standing well in a garden on a ridge. The better game viewing is down the road at Salt Lick, where the rooms are in an arc of inter-connected concrete mushrooms overlooking a pool. The pool is on the Bura, a permanent river, and a lot of game comes to water here in dry weather. Local residents appreciate the fact that these two lodges are outside a National Park and so no park fees are payable.

The next station on the railway is Bura, from which a road runs up into the Taita Hills via an old-established Catholic mission; the sister Protestant mission site is Wusi, in the next valley to the east, where Murray High School for girls is located. The main tarmac road up into the Taita Hills starts from further on, at Mwatate, and is worth taking if you have time for a visit. Soon after the turn you see Kenyatta High School, almost an oasis in its own right thanks to some enlightened tree planting by a former headmaster, Sammy Maneno. The whole distance from Mwatate to Wundanyi, the Taita administrative centre, is only 18 km (11 miles), and the change from the hot plain below to the cool 1500 metre (5000 feet) uplands is refreshing. Some of the hillsides are terraced and the *shambas* on the slopes seem to grow chiefly maize and bananas; there are also citrus, loquats and guavas. Off the tarmac the roads become mountain trails and the scenery is almost alpine. Not far from the foot of the hills there are deposits of precious stones, and rubies and grossular garnets are mined.

The Taita Hills cannot be said to be well signposted, and unless you are prepared to risk getting lost it is probably best to come down by the same road and head for Mwatate. From there it is a straightforward run of 24 km (15 miles), partly through bush and partly through sisal, to Voi.

Voi to Mombasa

The last 151 km (94 miles) of the Nairobi/Mombasa road is nowadays a two-hour run in a car. It is hard to realize that this country was such a formidable barrier to the old foot caravans. However, it involved a crossing of the Taru Desert, a stretch of several days' march with no surface water in the dry season. This type of land is called *nyika* (wilderness), and consists mainly of thorn bush, with some *commiphora* (easily recognizable by the shiny stems). It is sparkling green and bright with wild flowers just after the rains, but for most of the year it is dry and dusty, with much of the vegetation turning first brown and then nearly grey.

You pass the Sagala Hills to your right after leaving Voi. About 32 km (20 miles) beyond Voi you see the hill of Maungu on your right, where there is a water-hole; caravans used to make for it after crossing the Taru, and might have to go on as far as Voi if it was dry. The ranch on which Maungu hill lies has a big acreage of the jojoba bean—the bean which likes desert conditions and yields when crushed an oil that is an acceptable substitute for sperm whale oil. On the ranch and in the country between here and Kasigau, the 1500 metre (5000 feet) hill that dominates the landscape to the south, burial cairns are to be found with the bodies under them buried in a contracted position. Since cairn burials are a pastoralist custom of great antiquity, much practised by the Cushites and still carried on, these cairns may well mark the limits of Galla penetration in the first half of the 19th century.

Leave the Buchuma Gate of Tsavo East park on your left, and 66 km (41 miles) from Voi you reach Mackinnon Road, a British military installation during the Second World War and a supply base for some time after it. It now has few residents. The name comes from Sir William Mackinnon, the chairman of the British India shipping line who was the chief founder of the Imperial British East Africa Company in 1888.

By the time you reach Samburu the country begins to look less parched and a few palm trees appear. Mariakani, 119 km (74 miles) from Voi, has a large milk-collecting centre. Roads from here branch off southwards to Kinango and northwards to Kilifi and Malindi. You are now in the country of the Mijikenda, the peoples of the Nine Villages. The homeland of these nine Bantu-speaking groups is the long stretch of low hills and high ground running parallel to the coast and a few miles inland both north and south of Mombasa.

15 km (9 miles) beyond Mariakani is Mazeras, where there is a botanical garden open to the public. The turning to the left will take you by a road that is often rough to Rabai, 5 km (3 miles) away, and to Ribe, about 10 km (6 miles) further. It was at Rabai that Johann Ludwig Krapf, the Lutheran missionary employed by the Church Missionary Society, started the first inland Christian mission in 1846. The first church which Krapf and his colleague Rebmann built was superseded after a decade or two, but the second church on the site, completed in 1879 and still standing, is thought to be the oldest Christian church in Kenya.

Krapf had to leave East Africa because of ill health in 1853, but he returned ten years later to help Wakefield and the Methodists to establish their new station. This was located at Ribe on Krapf's advice; in recent years the Ribe hilltop has been the site of a teachers' college and a school. Rebmann continued working at Rabai for many years and was found there, blind and in the company of only a few converts, by Sir Bartle Frere in 1873. Frere, after his service as a governor in India, was the British Government's anti-slavery emissary. It was in the next year that the Church Missionary Society, with Frere's blessing, obtained the land to the north of Mombasa on which they established their settlement for freed slaves.

From Mazeras there is an easy descent of 17 km (10.5 miles) through Changamwe to the Makupa Causeway and on to Mombasa Island.

Places to stay

Kiboko
Hunter's Lodge

Kibwezi
Bushwhackers (self-help)

Mtito Andei
Tsavo Inn

Tsavo West
Kilaguni Lodge
Kitani Lodge (self-help)
Ngulia Lodge
Ngulia Safari Camp (self-help)

Tsavo East
Aruba Lodge (self-help)
Voi Safari Lodge
Tsavo Safari Camp
Crocodile Camp

Namanga
Namanga River Hotel

Amboseli
Amboseli Lodge
Amboseli Serena Lodge
Ol Tukai Lodge (self-help)
Kilimanjaro Buffalo Lodge
Kilimanjaro Safari Lodge

Taita Hills
Taita Hills Lodge
Salt Lick Lodge

Mountain climbing and walking

Lukenya

Fishing

Dam on the Kiboko River
(Hunter's Lodge)

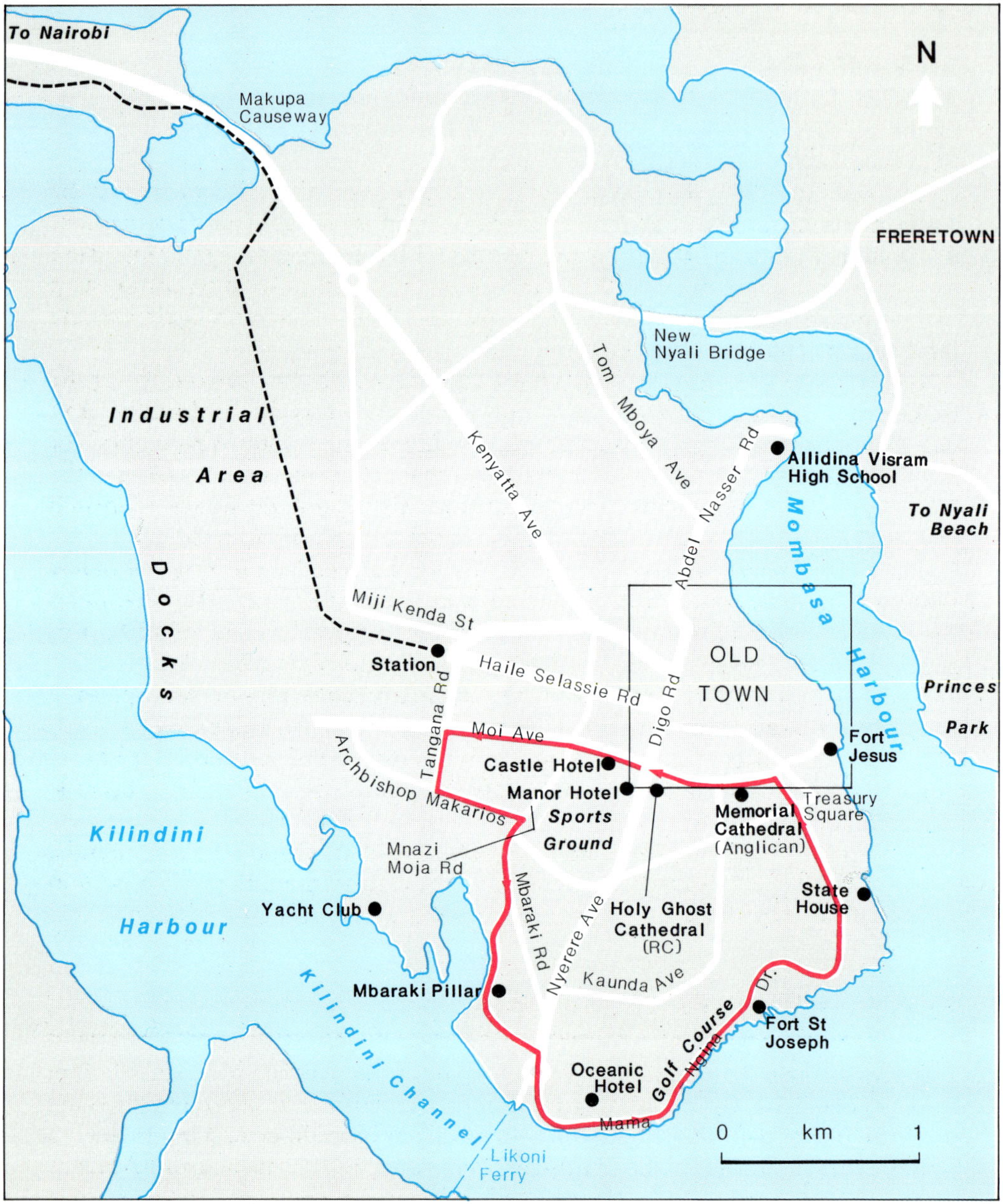

Mombasa Island

5 The Coast

Kenya's coastal strip, the ribbon of green lying between the dry country and the sea, is not wide. Down near the Tanzanian boundary the arid lands come close to the shore; opposite Mombasa and Malindi there are trees and grass for 50 km (30 miles) or so inland; north of the Tana River and into Somalia the strip widens out, despite a lower rainfall, but further north it narrows again and the land is arid almost to the sea.

The western edge of this strip, where it merges into the dry country, is the home of a small population of peoples who live mainly by hunting and gathering berries, edible greenery, roots and honey. The Waliangulu (or Sanye) hunters of the Tana region operate along the north-eastern fringes of the Taru. The Boni live north-east of Lamu on the mainland in semi-forested thicket country. These hunters are some of the earliest inhabitants.

The central part of the coastal zone at its southern end is the long line of low hills running from south to north which you crossed between Mariakani and Mazeras on the road from Nairobi. This is the home of the group of Bantu-speaking agriculturalists called the Mijikenda (Nine Villages).

Another Bantu people, the Pokomo, occupy and cultivate the flood-plain of the Tana River. Still another Bantu group, the Bajun people, who are fishermen as well as farmers, live on the mainland and islands north of Lamu. Some of these groups still follow traditional religions while others have become Christian or Muslim.

The eastern edges of the coastal strip, the coastal plain and off-shore islands, are where the Swahili and Arabs live; they have traditionally made homes in towns and farmed the countryside round about. Their religion is Islam.

Early visitors and immigrants

The Kenya coast has been part of the Indian Ocean trading zone since before the time of Christ. Greek sailors from Egypt learned how to sail down the coast with the north-east monsoon, which blows from November to March, and to return with the onset of the south-east monsoon, which blows from April to October. So far as we know they traded, mainly iron goods against ivory, but did not settle.

The merchants from Arabia and the Persian Gulf who came to the coast from the 8th century AD onwards were not all birds of passage. Some of them settled and intermarried with the local black population. The earliest such settlement so far excavated is Manda, on Manda Island, dating from the 9th century.

By the early Middle Ages there was a negroid population all along the seaboard from the Zambezi in the south to Mogadishu in the north. Arab geographers called it the Land of Zanj (as in Zanzibar), the land of black men. Along the East African coast the mixing of immigrants with these people had produced over the years a unique African culture—Swahili. It blended local with imported ideas on dress, food and social behaviour. It was Islamic by religion but Bantu by language.

The halcyon period of this Swahili culture was between the 13th and 15th centuries, by which time there were 37 towns along the coast from Mogadishu in the north to Kilwa, south of Dar es Salaam. In 1498 Vasco da Gama called at Mombasa and Malindi, and within a few years the Portuguese had taken over the east coast gold trade and were demanding tribute from the towns along the seaboard; Kilwa and Mombasa resisted and were sacked. Portugal completed her conquest by 1506 and the Swahili coastal towns declined.

From Vasco da Gama to Jomo Kenyatta

Portuguese rule lasted for 200 years despite various hazards. In the mid-16th century the coast was raided several times by the Turks. Later, a cannibal horde called the Zimba, starting on the rampage from their home on the Zambezi, had killed and eaten their way up the coast until by 1547 they had destroyed Kilwa. They sacked Mombasa, then laid siege to Malindi. Suddenly they were attacked from the rear by the warriors of the Segeju people, who were moving southwards along the coast at this time. Malindi was saved and most of the Zimba were killed.

Portugal saw that it was unwise to rely on Malindi's goodwill to safeguard the passage to India. To strengthen the north coast administration and defences, she began the construction of Fort Jesus at Mombasa in 1593.

The appearance of the Segeju as a relieving force at Malindi was in fact a result of upheavals in the interior. During the 16th century there had been a big expansion by the Galla people into southern Somalia and Kenya from their homeland in south-eastern Ethiopia. A number of African peoples—Taita, Pokomo, Mijikenda, Segeju—claim that their ancestors came to their present homes from an area called Shungwaya in southern Somalia, from which they were expelled by the Galla. The ancestors of the Taita people eventually came to rest in the Taita Hills. The Pokomo settled along the lower Tana. The Mijikenda occupied their plateau and coastal range of hills inland of Mombasa. The Segeju, who together with the Digo group of the Mijikenda had been the first to leave Shungwaya, finally settled down on the Tanzanian border. During this time destruction was widespread, and many towns along the north coast were temporarily abandoned.

It was the Omani Arabs who eventually succeeded in driving out the Portuguese. Muscat, their capital, was one of the key points on the route to India controlled by Portugal. But in 1650 the Arabs under their Imam managed to expel them. Thereupon Mombasa requested the Omanis to help in expelling the Portuguese from East Africa as well, and a small naval force in 1652 responded by raiding Pate and Zanzibar and killing the Portuguese they found there. For 40 years there was a series of attempts by Mombasa and the towns of the Lamu archipelago to eject the Portuguese with Omani help, followed inevitably by reprisals at various times against Lamu, Pate, Faza, Siyu, Manda and Mombasa itself. In 1696 the Imam moved a big fleet to Mombasa island and besieged Fort Jesus. After dogged resistance that lasted until December 1698 the defenders were overcome. From that time until 1963, with only a brief interlude in 1728–9 when Portugal staged a short-lived comeback, the fort was in fact or in theory under Omani Arab control.

Early in the 18th century, Oman started appointing *liwali*, i.e. governors, to the East African coastal towns. Control of Mombasa came into the hands of the Mazrui family, the first Mazrui having begun as deputy governor in 1727. But in practice the Omanis exerted little control and the towns were virtually independent.

But when the Busaidi dynasty came to power in Oman, things changed. After the first Busaidi Imam died in 1784 there was a succession struggle during which the pretender tried to turn Oman's African possessions into an independent state. Zanzibar, though besieged, held out and eventually handed itself over to the relieving force of the legitimate ruler. At the turn of the 19th century, when the Omani rulers paid more attention to East Africa, it was on loyalist Zanzibar that their efforts were concentrated. In addition to her traditional market for ivory, beeswax and tortoiseshell, Zanzibar now handled a greatly increased trade in slaves, required to work the sugar plantations of the French Indian Ocean islands. The commercial position of Zanzibar became so important to the Omanis that in 1840 Seyyid Said, the most outstanding of the Busaidi rulers, moved his court from Muscat to the island.

As Zanzibar rose, Mombasa declined. The Mazrui had seized control of Pemba about 1750 and used its rice to increase Mombasa's food supply. Early in the 19th century, taking advantage of a dynastic dispute in Pate, the incumbent Mazrui led an expedition to the town and installed his own nominee as sultan. In 1813, with troops from Pate assisting his own Mombasa men, he attempted to take Lamu also. This time he went too far. The soldiers of Lamu, showing unexpected courage and skill, met the invaders at the battle of Shela and threw them back in the sea.

Fort Jesus

For Pate the Shela defeat was crushing. But the reaction of Mombasa was an assertion of independence in 1814, and an appeal to Bombay for the protection of Great Britain. This was refused. Another such appeal was made in 1824 to Captain Owen, who called at Mombasa in HMS Leven just when Seyyid Said's fleet was bombarding the Mazrui in Fort Jesus. Thinking Mombasa would be a useful centre from which to counter the slave trade, Owen granted the request and raised the Union Jack over the fort. He sent off a dispatch explaining what he had done and then sailed on, leaving a detachment ashore under Lt Reitz. Reitz died soon after, and command was then exercised by young midshipmen until the British Government repudiated Owen's agreement and the first British protectorate ended in 1826.

Seyyid Said at once demanded the submission of the Mazrui; they made a peace treaty with him which they broke whenever his back was turned. In 1837 Said managed to arrest leading members of the Mazrui family and send them to exile in the Persian Gulf; only two younger members of the family were allowed to remain as subordinate governors, one at Takaungu on the north coast and the other at Gazi on the south. In 1840 Said made his move to Zanzibar and lived and ruled there, apart from one short visit to Muscat, until he died in 1856. The effective independence of Mombasa and most of the Kenya coast towns thus came to an end.

Seyyid Said's enterprise gave a strong impetus to East African trade. Europe wanted to buy more ivory, vegetable oils and gum copal. There was a continuing demand for slaves from Arabia, and Said's policy of developing agriculture—he introduced the clove industry into Zanzibar and Pemba—led to a growing demand along the coast for slave labour to work the plantations.

Mombasa was slow to share in the growing prosperity. Its population was down to about 3000 in the 1840s. Traditionally trade was brought to Mombasa by others; its citizens did not go out and generate it. Slaves were brought to the town from Kilwa and Zanzibar and resold for onward shipment to Lamu and the north. Kamba and Chagga sources provided the ivory that was Mombasa's chief export. Mijikenda traders were often the intermediaries and they provided much of the town's food after it lost its Pemba granary to Zanzibar in 1823. They used to meet Swahili agents at recognized border markets such as Kwa Jomvu. However, relations between Mombasa and the Mijikenda cooled after the Zanzibari take-over in 1837. Agents were no longer appointed, and much of the Mijikenda trade was switched to Gazi and Takaungu, where it continued into the present century.

The up-country commerce of the coast was interrupted in the 1840s and 1850s by the raiding of the Kwavi Maasai and their wars with the pastoral Maasai. When the Kwavi menace was removed Mombasa flourished again. By 1860 the flow of trade had changed direction, and large well-armed caravans led by Arab and Swahili traders were already making long safaris inland to buy their own ivory and slaves.

Fishermen returning with catch. The line of foam marks the off-shore reef.

The overseas trade in slaves was gradually suppressed and the Zanzibar slave market closed in 1873. One result was a boom in the agriculture of Kenya's north coast as more cheap slave labour became available and the Swahilis extended their plantations of cereals and coconuts. Some demand for slaves continued through the later 19th century, and even during the 1890s when the railway designed to stop slavery was actually being built, its surveyors found Arab and Swahili caravans still operating in the interior. But by the turn of the century the slave trade was dead.

There were two serious challenges to the rule of the Busaidi sultans. A long-lasting one came from Mbarak, the young son of the last Mazrui ruler of Mombasa, who had been permitted to live and rule at Gazi. After half a lifetime of attempted rebellion in 1882 he managed to raise a considerable force of 2000 men from the local people and the Maasai and led them in an attack on Vanga. The Sultan's army under its commander, a British naval officer called Lloyd Mathews, surrounded Mbarak's stronghold and took it by storm. Mbarak escaped but eventually gave himself up. He was allowed to return to Gazi and caused no more trouble.

The other challenge arose on the island of Pate, where the Sultan had built a fort at Siyu in the 1850s. A force led by a member of the Pate ruling house, Ahmad, later known as Simba (Lion), ejected the building's defenders and destroyed it. When the Sultan's troops returned and rebuilt the fort, Simba moved to the mainland and established himself in a fortified forest stronghold at Witu. Here he managed in the course of time to build up an independent sultanate.

At the time of the Scramble for Africa two decades later Simba appealed for German protection, and in 1887 a German Witu Company was set up. But by the Anglo-German agreement of 1890, which partitioned East Africa into German and British zones of operation, Witu fell within the British sphere and the German company withdrew. However, the IBEA (Imperial British East Africa) Company had difficulty in taking over, since Sultan Simba had rallied behind him the Arab landowners of the north coast who saw their livelihood threatened by Zanzibar's anti-slavery policy. After a short but expensive occupation the IBEA Company had also to withdraw in 1893. The Sultan's army then moved in and took Witu, demolishing its defences. Sultan Simba escaped but was later caught and executed.

In 1895 company rule gave way to colonial rule. Great Britain declared a protectorate over the territories that later became Kenya and Uganda. A 16-km (10-mile) strip along the Kenya coast was recognized as being part of the Sultan of Zanzibar's domains and he was paid an annual rent for it; the red flag of Oman still flew over Fort Jesus; and when Kenya became a Crown Colony, this strip remained a protectorate.

The rule of the Busaidi dynasty came to an end with the Zanzibar revolution of January 1964. The Sultan went into exile in England, and an African government assumed control of Zanzibar and Pemba. One month before, in December 1963, an African government had taken over from the British colonial administration in Nairobi. The coastal strip which had belonged to Zanzibar for so long became an integral part of the newly independent Kenya.

Mombasa

The centre of modern Mombasa is the crossroads where Moi Avenue runs into Nkrumah Road and where Nyerere Avenue becomes Digo Road. This is where buses from the mainland hotels drop their passengers, either at the Manor Hotel a few metres south of the crossing or at the Castle a little way west of it. If you prefer to see the town on foot, here are two walks that start from this point. The first, northwards towards the Old Harbour, is suitable for the early morning before the day gets too hot. The second, south towards the modern harbour of Kilindini (at the Deep Water), is a much longer walk for the afternoon and evening.

North of Mombasa town centre

Set off along Digo Road and turn right after the General Post Office into Makadara Road. As you walk eastwards down Makadara Road the boundary of the Old Town is the left side of the street. On your right is Jamhuri (Republic) Park, and the first place of worship in it to your right is the Baluchi Mosque. Baluchi soldiers were some of the regular troops employed by the Imam and the Omani governors, and took part in the siege of Fort Jesus in 1696–8. On the far side is the Hindu Temple of Lord Shiva. At the end of the park on your right is the Mbaruk Mosque, an Arab foundation dating from about 1870.

Follow Makadara Road round to its junction with Nkrumah Road, then turn left with the Bank of India to your left and the old Law Courts on your right. The curving entrance to Fort Jesus is a little further down the hill.

The fort is now a national museum and deserves an unhurried visit if you can spare the time. It is a superb example of late fortification architecture, and the museum on the site of some of the old barracks is rewarding. Much of the fort is open to the public and it is best to buy James Kirkman's guide and wander round at leisure. A Portuguese frigate, the *Santo Antonio*, was wrecked off the fort in 1697 and divers have recovered a lot of material, some of which is displayed in the museum.

As you leave the fort you are facing the old town and access to Ndia Kuu (Main Street) is just across the road. This part adjacent to Fort Jesus was

Mombasa Old Town

formerly the walled town built by the Portuguese. The north-westerly part, still overlooking the dhow harbour, was the old Swahili town, Mvita.

This quarter of Mombasa is a warren of narrow streets and alleys with here and there a carved wooden balcony on a house or a carved door, some of the best of them being on mosques. Most of the women in the streets are shrouded in their black *buibuis* (spiders). Many of the men wear long white *kanzus* and *kofias* (caps). There is a variety of pungent smells, some pleasant and some not. Many of the shops and offices are dark, but serious business is still done in them.

Turn right and walk down Mbarak Hinawy Road past the entrance to Mombasa Club. The Mandhry Mosque in this street is reputed to be the oldest on the island, dating from about 1570. The Old Customs House is on your right next to the entrance to the Old Harbour jetty. Even after the Second World War it was a good sight in the dhow season, with rugs and brass-studded chests piled in heaps against the walls. But nowadays the dhow traffic has dwindled to a remnant; the main north-bound cargo, mangrove-poles for building, has been less in demand since Arabia could afford to build in concrete.

Go past the Fish Market next door and proceed to the junction with Ndia Kuu. Turn left up the lower part of this street and then right into Old Kilindini Road. Passing an Ismaili mosque, cross over Kibokoni Road and have a look at the Basheikh Mosque on your right, which has good doors at the side. It is one of the oldest mosques in the town, but its date is uncertain; by tradition it was a Swahili foundation.

The next crossroad after the Basheikh Mosque is Rogers Road. Turn right down it, and bear right at the junction with Nehru Road. The next turning on your left is Biashara (Business) Street, a long road which crosses Digo Road and runs west; it has some good shops, especially in its western sector, and a heart-of-the-bazaar atmosphere, rather like Biashara Street in Nairobi.

If you want to walk further, take the next turn left down Kuze Road to Mlango wa Papa (Shark's Gate) Road, then right as far as you can go. The

Brass-studded Arab chest

beaches near here are where dhows used to be careened. A left turn into Mzizima Road will take you out on to Abdel Nasser Road, and this will lead you back into Digo Road. Notice the Allidina Visram High School to the north on the promontory overlooking the old port. It commemorates a remarkable Asian businessman who started in Tanzania in 1877, supplying caravans going up-country, and who gradually expanded the business until his network of shops and trading posts covered the three East African mainland territories. He was a pioneer of the Uganda cotton industry, and died in 1916.

If you prefer a shorter walk, first see as much of the Biashara Street shops as you want to, then go south along Digo Road. The municipal vegetable market is on your left, with a good place next to it for buying straw hats and baskets. A left turn will then take you into Langoni Road. The Jain Temple, one of Mombasa's more beautiful Hindu places of worship, is just off this street.

Return to Digo Road, cross it, and after you pass the Post Office turn right down Khalid Street. The Sheikh Jundani Mosque, standing well and adorned with an occasional palm tree, dates from about 1870. The Splendid Hotel serves an oriental meal in its roof restaurant.

Moi Avenue lies a short step to the south along Msanifu Kombo Street. The Tototo Shop is on the left down this street just before the junction. It is a non-profit making centre, run by the National Christian Council of Kenya, selling craft work of good quality at fair prices. At the corner with Moi Avenue you see the Castle Hotel across the road and turn left to your starting-point.

Sheikh Jundani Mosque, Mombasa

South of Mombasa Town Centre

Start again from the junction of Moi Avenue, Digo Road, Nkrumah Road and Nyerere Avenue. On the south-west corner here, by the way, is City House, where the British Council up on the first floor runs a respectable library. This time your route is westwards along Moi Avenue, past the Castle Hotel, the Mistral Restaurant and the Kenya Coffee House, under the Council's ornamental tusks and past Uhuru (Independence) Gardens. Note and use if necessary the Information Bureau next to the gardens—the staff are helpful and well-informed.

The next stretch of the avenue has the Bella Vista Restaurant, the Kenya Airways office and the offices of various travel agents and car hire firms. When you come to the Tangana Road crossroads, turn left. Right here would take you to the railway station. Straight on leads you past the Hong Kong Chinese restaurant a block and a half further along, and then to the port.

Proceed southwards along Tangana Road. If you crossed the railway at the end and turned right you would come to the Kilindini Mosque, a renewal on the site of an older mosque dating probably from the later 17th century. This is the area of Kilindini Town, where a group of Swahili immigrants, the so-called Three Tribes (of Kilindini, Tangana and Changamwe), arrived in Portuguese times and set up a separate settlement on the south side of the island. Their descendants are said to have abandoned Kilindini and moved across to Mombasa Town in 1837. Straight on after the railway would lead you to the Yacht Club and the Outrigger Hotel, where there are deep-sea fishing facilities.

Turn left along Archbishop Makarios Road and follow it to its junction with Mnazi Moja (One Coconut) Road. Turn right, leaving the cluster of sports clubs and their grounds to your left. After Mnazi Moja becomes Mbaraki Road, notice on your right the Little Theatre Club, Mombasa's main centre of amateur drama. Fork right before you reach the Railway Sports Club and follow the shoreline of Mbaraki Creek as far as the leaning Mbaraki Pillar, built about AD 1700 and still used as a centre for communication with the spirit world. The ruined mosque next to it was abandoned about AD 1500.

The left turn after the Pillar will take you to the far end of Nyerere Avenue. Turn right as though heading for the Likoni Ferry, then take the left fork at the roundabout. Leave the bus terminal on your right and follow the road through the old baobab trees to the edge of the Kilindini channel.

This walk round the southern sea front is Mombasa's favourite place to get an evening breeze and the early part through the public gardens can be crowded. The first stretch in front of the Oceanic Hotel is the site of another early settlement called Tuaca, occupied probably from the 12th to the 15th century. Its date and the identity of the builders are not known. The Oceanic, which runs a casino, must have one of the best sites on the island.

The Tusks, Moi Avenue, Mombasa, after rain

Follow the road round past the New Florida night club and casino and between the fairways of Mombasa Golf Course. The low walls at the cliff edge to your right where the road bends inland are reputed to be the scanty remains of Fort St Joseph, a Portuguese defensive work later rebuilt by the Arabs.

The road continues past the club-house and round the headland of Ras Serani, past Police HQ and State House, the President's coastal residence. After Mombasa Hospital and the Provincial Headquarters you emerge into Treasury Square, with its pleasant garden and shade trees. The ornamental bust is of Allidina Visram. The cool offices on the seaward side of the square include District Headquarters and the Town Hall.

At the far end of the square a left turn will take you into Nkrumah Road and past the Anglican Cathedral. Ambalal House, further down, houses the Capri Restaurant and a coffee shop as well as the Cave night club. The Catholic Cathedral of the Holy Ghost is on your left just before you return to your starting point at the junction with Nyerere Avenue.

The south mainland

Follow Nyerere Avenue from the middle of Mombasa and leave the island by the Likoni Ferry. Look to starboard as you cross the channel and you will see the berths of Kilindini Harbour on the north shore. Along the south shore you can see the old house of Sir Ali bin Salim, a former *Liwali* (the sultan's local governor) of the Coast, and probably a naval vessel off Mtongwe beyond. Further inland is Port Reitz, a surprisingly large area of deep water with many creeks running off it.

A left turn at the top of the slope after the ferry would take you to Shelly Beach, the first of the south coast hotels, and the Tibwani camp site. The road continues south through small *shambas* (cultivated plots) and villages with plenty of trees: coconut palms are frequent, there is the occasional kapok, and most of the villages have mangoes. Look at the roofs. Most of them are tin or thatch, but here and there you see examples of *makuti*, the traditional coast roof made with tiles of sewn palm-leaves, very cool and effective. Since the tiles are light, big spans are possible and many coast hotels have made beautiful use of *makuti* roofs.

The next beach along the coast is Tiwi, and signs to the places you can stay there appear on the main road before you come to Tiwi itself, which is 22 km (14

The Coast south of Mombasa

miles) from Mombasa. There are various groups of cottages to rent along the northern part of Tiwi Beach, notably El Capricho and Maweni. The Twiga Lodge cottages and camping ground are on the southern part of the beach.

At the mouth of the Tiwi River is the Kongo Mosque, an abandoned 18th century building in a fair state of preservation. It is on the south bank, so in order to reach it you have to go on through Tiwi village and across the river, then turn left at the sign for Diani Police Station. After about 400 metres you turn right, then bear left for the rest of the way.

The next beach, Diani, is the principal beach of the south coast. The main road of access to it is a tarmac left turn just before Ukunda. Ukunda, the small shopping centre and post office for the Diani area, is 6 km (4 miles) beyond Tiwi.

If you take the left turn you reach a T-junction just short of the sea, and from there a tarmac road runs north and south, parallel to the main road and the shore, serving the Diani Beach hotels and houses. Northwards, to the left, are a cluster of hotels with splendid sand in front of them, Diani Sea Lodge, Diani Reef, Golden Beach, Leopard Beach and Leisure Lodge, with particularly well laid-out gardens and a casino. Many coast hotels, including some of these, are served by regular tours from Europe.

As you go south there is nearly 1.5 km (about 1 mile) of foreshore where the shore-line is coral and there is very little sand. The beach becomes sandy again and good for bathing just before Trade Winds Hotel and continues like this past the Two Fishes, Africana Sea Lodge, Jadini and Nomad Beach Tented Hotel to the Robinson Baobab on a small promontory. After this come the cottages of Four Twenty South and the sandy Galu Beach.

Continue southwards down the main road through Ukunda. The next village, about 7 km (4.5 miles) further on, is Mwabungo, where a minor road turns off right towards the Shimba Hills and there are cashew nut plantations. Go straight on, and between Mwabungo and Gazi Bay you pass Kinondo, which has been an important area for the Digo people, the most southerly of the Mijikenda. Each people of the Mijikenda originally had a central walled village, known as a *kaya*, up in the low range of hills to the west. The principal village of the Wadigo was at Kwale, but some time after its foundation a group of settlers moved on and founded a second main *kaya* at Kinondo.

The road then curves inland round the bay until you reach the loop road to Gazi itself, the village which was the old Mazrui stronghold of the rebel Mbarak. His house in the village still stands and is reputed to be haunted. About 5 km (3 miles) south of Gazi is the Msambweni turn-off, which leads to a district branch hospital. The hospital is close to another long sandy beach. On the cliffs about 3 km (2 miles) to the north is a rather dull stone ruin, thought to have been a slave-pen of Mbarak's.

As you go south you begin to see fields of sugar cane until 16 km (10 miles) beyond Msambweni you reach Ramisi and its sugar factory. 3 km (2 miles) or so beyond Ramisi is a turning to the left which brings you after another 10 km (6 miles) to the fishing village of Shimoni (At the Hole). Shimoni is the home of the Pemba Channel Fishing Club, a noted centre for deep-sea fishing. The Hole refers to a local network of caves, one entrance to which is close to the Fishing Club turn-off.

Off Shimoni is Wasini Island, said to have been settled originally by families from down the coast who had tired of raids by Kwavi Maasai and wanted somewhere more peaceful to live. South again of Wasini are the small islands of Mpunguti and Kisiti which are a Marine National Park. The snorkelling here is said to be the finest on the Kenya coast. If you do not want the trouble of hiring a boat, calculating the state of the tides and so on, you can make an excursion to the park with Thorn Tree Safaris.

Continue down the main road from Ramisi towards the Tanzanian border. After about 16 km (10 miles) a road joins you from the right near Mrima Hill, which has deposits of rare earths. The road continues past occasional patches of forest, with Segeju country to your left, the present home of the people who relieved the Portuguese at Malindi in 1587. 99 km (59 miles) from Mombasa you reach Lunga Lunga, the Kenya border post. A left turn just after the village will take you down the valley of the Umba River to the small port and fishing village of Vanga. Be careful, by the way, if you come here on a bus; the buses from Mombasa stop overnight and return in the morning, but Vanga has no hotel of the standard preferred by visitors.

From Lunga Lunga retrace your steps back up the main road for 3 km (2 miles), then take the turning to the left inland to Kinango. This road passes through a long stretch of pleasant but not very interesting landscape, first through Digo country, then through country of the Duruma people, another Mijikenda group. The Duruma keep cattle and Kinango is a collecting centre for milk. From it a road runs north to Mariakani and the milk depot. Your road is the one that leads eastwards to Kwale.

The first half of the run from Kinango to Kwale is dull; the second half is beautiful. The road winds through forest up into the Shimba Hills and passes through the northern part of the Shimba Hills National Reserve. This game sanctuary is Kenya's principal home of the sable antelope, but it has quite a wide range of other game. Though only about 20 km (12 miles) long by 8 km (5 miles) wide, the reserve has elephant, buffalo, lion and leopard, hyena and various species of buck and monkey, though not in large numbers. The birds include carmine bee-eaters (a local migrant), eagles, spurfowl, crested guinea-fowl and the attractive little Zanzibar red bishop. There are camp sites and self-help *bandas* in the reserve, but no lodge.

To the left of the road about 3 km (2 miles) before the township and still in the reserve are the remains of the Early Iron Age settlement radiocarbon-dated to

Outrigger canoes with lateen sails

the 3rd century AD, after which the distinctive style of pottery called Kwale ware is named. From the Kwale District headquarters the road is an almost continuous gentle slope down to the main south coast road, which it joins north of Tiwi. You make a left turn for the short last lap to Likoni Ferry.

The north mainland to Kilifi

Take the northward route via Digo Road to leave Mombasa island by way of the Nyali Bridge. The last part of this route passes through an area which an oral tradition says was settled in medieval times before the Old Town was developed.

The church to your left as you drive on to the north mainland is Emmanuel Church, Freretown, built by freed slaves. Freretown was established in 1874 mainly to provide a home for slaves released by the British Navy from captured dhows and left with nowhere to go, having been driven from homes far in the interior. It was named after Sir Bartle Frere, the former Indian administrator who became the British Government's travelling agent for anti-slavery work. There is a portrait in the church of Matthew Wellington, one of the men who carried David Livingstone's body from Ilala to the coast; his is the best-known grave in the CMS (Church Missionary Society) cemetery near by. The church's bell-tower stands at the junction where the road from Nyali joins the

The Coast north of Mombasa

main road to Bamburi and the north. Its bell used to be rung hourly during the night to warn any slaving dhows in the channel that the settlement was on guard. Freretown was of course highly unpopular with the Arab owners of slave-worked plantations whose livelihood it was undermining; they organized attacks on the mission in 1880 and 1895.

A right turn on to the Nyali road would take you past the Bahari Club for deep-sea fishing to where the old pontoon bridge used to meet the mainland. On your right is the Tamarind Restaurant, well-sited and good for sea-food, and beyond it, past the cement silos, are the monument to Krapf—the CMS missionary who wrote the first Swahili dictionary—and the graves of Krapf's wife and daughter, who died in Mombasa in 1844 shortly after they arrived to start their mission. Beyond is Prince's Park with the Mombasa showground. The road inland near the old pontoon terminal leads round to a residential estate and Nyali Beach Hotel, one of the north coast's older and better hotels. The Nyali Golf Course is close by. Years of patient effort have removed the coral from the fairways and Nyali is now a very attractive 18-hole layout.

Your route is north from Nyali Bridge up the main road. The turning to the right after about 5 km (3 miles) leads round to Mombasa Beach Hotel, Mombasa Beach Apartments and the Reef Hotel. The Bahari Beach and Silver Beach Hotels are normally fully booked by overseas visitors.

The road runs quite near to the sea for the next stretch up to Shimo-la-Tewa. On the left is Bamburi Cement Factory; since coral is a form of limestone, the factory's raw material is all around it. Notice the skill with which a large quarried area here has been rehabilitated and turned into a park. To the right of the road Bamburi Beach is lined with hotels and cottages. Here are the Bamburi Beach, Whitesands, Ocean View and Kenya Beach Hotels, the Plaza—Severin Sea Lodge—Neptune group (the Neptune has a casino), the Cowrie Shell Apartments, and the Red Lobster Restaurant. The Dolphin and the New Coral/Palm Beach Hotels are usually fully booked. The Serena Beach Hotel is at the far northern end just before Cannon Point.

Immediately to the north of Shimo is the bridge over Mtwapa Creek. This is the home ground of Edward Rodwell's 'Coast Causerie', which readers of *The Standard* have long enjoyed. Two firms here cater for deep-sea fishing, goggling (snorkelling) and diving—F. G. MacConnel and Kenya Marinas. Le Pichet is a restaurant with French cuisine.

2 km (1.25 miles) up the coast north of the creek mouth are the Jumba Ruins, the remains of a fair-sized settlement with two mosques, some tombs, and a number of houses. The pottery dug from the site indicates that Jumba was inhabited from about AD 1350 to 1450.

Further up the coast road is the Portini Village Restaurant, which specializes in African food (mainly Swahili or Seychelles dishes). 7 km (4.5 miles) beyond Mtwapa are the turnings to the next beach, Kikambala. Here are the Kanamai

Holiday Centre of the National Christian Council of Kenya, Whispering Palms Hotel, the Bahari Cottages and the Sun 'n' Sand Hotel. At 36 km (24 miles) from Mombasa you reach Vipingo with its big sisal estate. 8 km (5 miles) before you reach Kilifi Creek a turn-off to the right from the village of Kibaoni leads to another small creek and the village of Takaungu, the northern base of the Mazruis after their expulsion from Mombasa in 1837. After the Takaungu turning the road passes through more hilly country and the farming land of Kilifi Plantations until the ramp to Kilifi Ferry is reached at 57 km (36 miles) from Mombasa.

As you go down the hill to the ferry there is a path to the left which leads to a small snake park and the ruins of an old settlement, partially excavated. To your right, also on the south bank of the creek, is the Mnarani Hotel, normally occupied by overseas visitors.

Kilifi township and the cashew-nut factory are on the north bank of the creek. The shops and the office of the DC, Kilifi District, lie between the main road and the sea. To the left of the road and a little further inland is the Sea Horse Hotel. The creek is a nice stretch of water which is visited annually by numbers of carmine bee-eaters.

For your return to Mombasa you have to retrace your route to the south of Kilifi Ferry for 4 km (2.5 miles) then branch off inland. This road climbs into the coastal range of hills and down part of the spine of Mijikenda country. You would meet two of the peoples of the Nine Villages, the Digo and the Duruma, on the south mainland. The traditional home of the Kauma group is to the west. South of them, in order, are five more groups whose traditional territory you now cross: the Chonyi, Jibana, Kambe, Ribe and Rabai. The most numerous of the Mijikenda, the Giriama, are the most northerly and have spread their agriculture furthest. You see Giriama women in their bulky skirts as far south as the Nairobi/Mombasa road and northwards well beyond the Sabaki River. Giriama girls often perform traditional dances in coast hotels.

The first township of any size that you come to is Kaloleni, where there are schools and a hospital. The original walled village of the Giriama, also called Giriama, was a little to the west of here. From Kaloleni the road to the south takes you through Ribe with its Methodist mission and Krapf's old mission station of Rabai to Mazeras. Turn left for the run down the hill into Mombasa.

Kilifi to Malindi

In the country north of Kilifi the main feature is the expanse of the Arabuko Sokoke Forest, which extends northwards to your left almost to the Sabaki River. There are not many tracks into it, but it is the home of certain animals not commonly found elsewhere, notably the yellow-rumped elephant shrew and a buck called Ader's duiker.

Serena Beach Hotel

Gedi

Two-thirds of the way to Malindi the road skirts Mida Creek, a wide stretch of shallow water and islands fringed in places with mangroves. The Tewa Caves near by, under water, have fair-sized fish in them, and the whole area is rich in birds. The best approach is not from the landward side but by boat from Watamu.

Soon after leaving the creek you come to a crossroads where the right turn takes you to Watamu. Just south-east of here is the ruined town of Gedi, which has largely been excavated and is a National Park. Large forest trees have grown up among the ruins and you can tour the park in shade. Buy a guidebook at the gate to learn what you are seeing and avoid getting lost. Gedi appears to have been a breakaway town from Malindi, or outlier to it, and was inhabited from the late 13th to the early 17th centuries. The most probable reason for its abandonment is the Galla raids of the latter period, though there are indications that its water supply may have begun to fail.

Watamu itself has good beaches, though seaweed is sometimes a problem, and a group of hotels. If you turn left when you near the sea you come to the Blue Lagoon; the Watamu Beach Hotel is normally fully booked by overseas visitors. A right turn will take you to Ocean Sports, Seafarers and the Turtle Bay Hotel. There is a Marine National Park here at Watamu and boat trips to it can be made from Ocean Sports or Seafarers.

Beyond the Gedi crossroads agriculture increases again. Notice that the local farmers, mainly Giriama, interplant cotton and maize in their fields. Shortly after the airfield, 15 km (9 miles) beyond Gedi, you enter Malindi.

The town, which is at least as old as the 13th century, has had a chequered history. It was very prosperous during the 15th century, and Vasco da Gama when he arrived was welcomed in some state by the ruling Arab sheikh. The population of the town was around 6000 people, and included a number of Indian merchants from Cambay who imported cotton cloth, glass, porcelain and beads, and exported such local products as ivory, rhino horn, tortoise-shell, gums and cowries. This good fortune continued all through the 16th century when the town was the base for Portuguese operations on this coast and a starting point for the voyage to India.

A decline set in when the local Portuguese headquarters was moved to Fort Jesus. It was hastened when the Galla raids of the later 17th century caused the temporary abandonment of the mainland towns on the north coast. A visiting Portuguese ship in the 18th century found the town dilapidated but still inhabited. However, by 1845, when Krapf visited it, Malindi was deserted.

The area was resettled by the Busaidi Sultan of Zanzibar in 1861 to serve as a granary for his dominions, and a thriving enterprise based on slave labour was built up. Maize and millet were exported and mangoes and coconuts grown. But by 1900 the enforcement of the ban on slavery had again crippled the economy. It has made a slow recovery during the present century with the introduction of agricultural settlement schemes, the encouragement of fishing, and the growth of tourism.

The few remaining historical monuments are within easy walking distance of the middle of town. Da Gama's Cross, first set up in 1499, stands at Vasco da Gama Point. There is a small Portuguese chapel just off the south road out to Silversands, part of which dates from the first half of the 16th century. Just inland from the sea front, near the big modern mosque, are two pillar tombs dated to the earlier 15th century. These pillar tombs are an unusual feature of the East African coast, and examples are found from Dar to the Somali border. There is another one, unfortunately fallen, at Mambrui to the north.

The beaches at Malindi are good, but after the rains the sea off the long northern beach is discoloured brown with mud brought down by the Sabaki River. It appears that the very heavy rains of 1961 changed the configuration of the sandbanks at the mouth and made Malindi more vulnerable. This is all the more to be regretted in that Malindi Bay, with no reef to shelter it, is one of the few places to offer very fair surfing when wind and sea are right.

As for accommodation, there are on Silversands, to the south of the town, Indian Ocean Lodge, the Driftwood Club, Silversands Beach Cottages and a camping site. To the south again, round Casuarina Point, are the boats in which you can visit the Malindi Marine National Park; both the Malindi and the Watamu parks are within a larger Malindi National Reserve in which a serious effort is being made to conserve the reef and its shells and fish.

On Malindi Bay, to the north, are Lawford's, the Blue Marlin, the Sindbad, the Eden Roc, the Suli Suli Club, and the Malindi Chalets. Further north, beyond the hotels, is a pleasant 9-hole golf course.

Malindi is an important north coast centre for deep-sea fishing. It has a Sea Fishing Club and firms which offer boats for charter. There is an annual sea-fishing festival. There are both a snake park and an aviary here. The aviary is a spacious affair called Birdland out on the south road past the Driftwood Club. The snake park is on the road to the north near Lawford's Hotel.

Most visitors who come to Malindi by road leave again by the main road to Mombasa. However, there are two routes by which you can by-pass Mombasa on a journey up-country, provided that the weather is dry. Take the road to the west inland through the Swahili village of Ganda to the Jilore Forest and the small centre of Kakoneni. 7 km (4.5 miles) after Kakoneni the road forks. The left fork is your first route to avoid Mombasa. It leads through the village of Kwa Dudu to the south, passes west of Vitengeni, then through Bamba until it reaches the Mombasa/Nairobi road at Mariakani.

The second route which you embark on when you take the right fork after Kakoneni is a track that goes up-stream along the course of the Galana/Sabaki River until it reaches Crocodile Camp and the Sala Gate into Tsavo East

A pillar tomb, Malindi

Vasco da Gama Point, Malindi

National Park about 100 km (62 miles) from Malindi. This road can be rough in parts and has patches that may be difficult to navigate when wet.

The Lamu Archipelago

Much of the visitors' traffic to places north of Malindi goes by air. This is basically because the Tana River has to be crossed, and during the two rainy seasons there may be too much water in the river for the ferry to operate; in a wet year, in fact, Lamu may be cut off by road from the south for weeks at a time. Nevertheless the journey by road has points of interest, and when the weather is dry there are regular bus services to Lamu, or rather to the mainland opposite Lamu Island, from Mombasa and Malindi.

Take the road to the north out of Malindi past the hotels along Malindi Bay. Cross the Sabaki River. The turning to the left after the bridge would take you through Marikebuni to the village of Marafa, 800 metres east of which is the Marafa Depression, alias Hell's Kitchen, a spectacular eroded valley. Your route is straight on, and 5 km (3 miles) north of the bridge you can if you wish make a detour to the right to visit Mambrui, as the buses do; it was a prosperous small Arab township at the end of the last century; the fallen pillar of its pillar tomb still has Ming porcelain bowls set into its upper part.

Return to the main road and head northwards towards Gongoni. The far end of the bay north of Mambrui has a good beach on which is Che Shale, a small lodge for deep-sea fishing and water sports which prides itself on its sea-food; the access road to it is restricted to 4-wheel drive vehicles. North of Che Shale and east of Gongoni is a peninsula on which stand the ancient ruins and the modern fishing village of Ngomeni. In Formosa Bay to the north, the Italians in 1966 set up a platform to launch satellites for space research.

Beyond Gongoni there is a long, dull stretch of road through bush until the Tana is reached at Garsen, 111 km (69 miles) north of Malindi. The township is a cosmopolitan trading centre used by Orma, the Galla pastoralists whose grazing grounds are to the north-west, by Pokomo farmers from up-stream, and Somali cattlemen from the north-east. Further up the Tana from Garsen, between here and Galole (Hola), is the Tana River Primate National Reserve, where red colobus and crested mangabey live in the riverine forest. There is a lodge to stay in, Baomo Lodge, bookings for which are mostly made through the Malindi hotels. The lodge is 160 km (100 miles) north of Malindi.

Once across the river the road runs east-south-east, and there are a few swampy patches which are difficult after heavy rain. 45 km (28 miles) after Garsen you reach Witu and the territory of the old 19th century sultanate; there are ruins of a palace of the sultan a few kilometres out along the Kipini road. The main road then skirts the remains of the Witu Forest and follows a wide arc round the bay in which Lamu Island lies until it reaches the coast again at Mokowe. This is where you leave your car or bus and take a boat for the trip across to the Lamu waterfront.

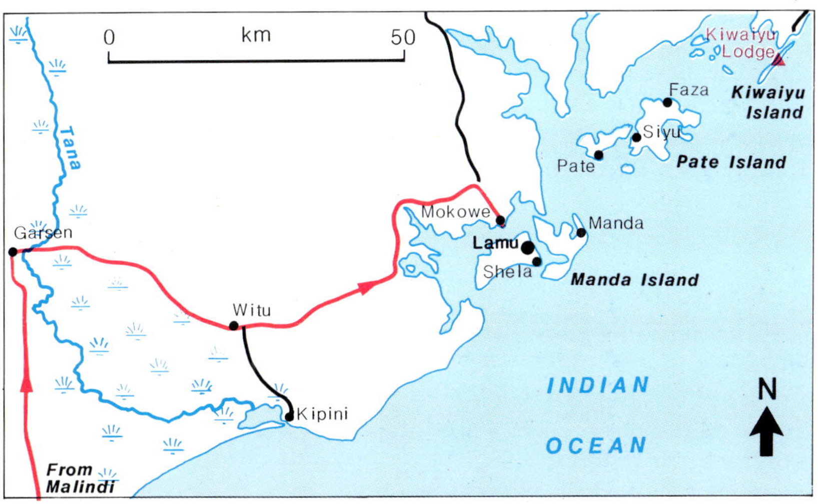

The Lamu Archipelago

The mainland between Witu and Lamu had a flourishing plantation agriculture in the later 19th century. Here again the abolition of slavery helped to cripple the economy. Government-aided settlement schemes are now reviving agriculture in the district, but earlier in this century some interesting Kenya characters farmed around Witu. One was Charles Whitton, known for many years as Coconut Charlie, a generous benefactor of the museum in Fort Jesus. Another was Percy Petley, who started Petley's Inn in Lamu. A third was Henri Bernier, the Swiss farmer whose house at Shela, along the coast from Lamu, was the nucleus of the Peponi Hotel.

Lamu is a peaceful old Arab and Swahili town, with narrow streets whose traffic is limited to pedestrians and donkeys; motorcars and bicycles are banned. The waterfront is lined with spacious two-storey houses, the old DC's house in the middle now being the Lamu Museum. Petley's Inn is close by. The New Mahrus Hotel is a little way inland. The fort, originally built around 1812 by the Omani Arabs, is now used as a prison and is not to be photographed. It is on a square off the main street, which runs parallel with the waterfront one block inland. One of the town's chief attractions is its carved wooden doors, to be seen still on many houses. The craft is not dead and the doors are still being made.

But primarily Lamu is a Muslim town, a centre of Islamic learning and something of a holy city. There are more than twenty mosques, and the Riyadah Mosque is the home of an annual festival held during the last week of the month of the Prophet's birth. Pilgrims come to it from all over East Africa and beyond. The Kenya coast is part of the Muslim world, and good manners require that Muslim ideas of decorum should be respected. This is especially true of Lamu. Large expanses of bare western flesh give offence to local feelings, and it matters that you should take care to be adequately covered in public.

3 km (2 miles) south along the island's shoreline is Peponi Hotel, a comfortable place on the edge of the village of Shela. The wind is *pepo* in Swahili, and *peponi*, literally 'in the breeze', is a normal Swahili term for paradise.

Shela itself was a prosperous town in the first half of the 19th century, and a number of Arab plantation owners had their homes here. They have long since departed, and the place is now a small Bajun fishing village. But there are ruins of some of the old stone houses decorated with ornamental plaster work. The Friday Mosque, built in 1829 and restored in 1948, is the outstanding building that survives. It was the battle on the beach at Shela in 1813, when the army of Lamu defeated the forces of Pate and their Mombasa allies, that started the decline of the Mazrui dynasty.

The island across the harbour from the Lamu waterfront is Manda. On it are the Lamu airfield and the Ras Kitau Hotel, an Italian enterprise. On the south-east coast is the cleared site of Takwa, a settlement that was founded about AD

1500 and abandoned, probably because of a falling water-table, about 1700. It has the ruins of a Great Mosque and a pillar tomb. The settlement of Manda, in the north-east of the island, was excavated by Neville Chittick in 1966. It has at present the distinction of being the oldest known town on the coast, the earliest remains having been dated to the 9th century AD. It was abandoned early in the 19th century when its wells dried up.

The other main historical sites of the archipelago are on the island of Pate, some distance to the north-east. To visit them usually involves, as with Manda, a boat trip through the Mkanda Channel between Manda Island and the mainland, and since the tide has to be fairly full for this channel to be navigable, a visit requires planning. There is a public boat service to Pate Island from Lamu, but it is designed to serve the homes of the present inhabitants rather than the ruins of those of their predecessors. There are no hotels of visitors' standard to stay in. Any serious visiting of the archaeological sites on Pate is best done by hiring a boat in Lamu with an experienced boatman.

The main settlement was of course Pate itself, at the south-west corner of the island, a place with a more distinguished history than any other in the archipelago. Its Nabhani sultans had ruled there since the 13th century, and in the late 18th century it produced some impressive Swahili literature. Siyu and its fort, whose capture by Zanzibar in the 1860s led to Ahmad crossing to the mainland and becoming Sultan Simba of the Witu Sultanate, are mid-way across the island. To the south of them, on the south coast, are the ruins of Shanga, now being examined. Faza, the present administrative centre, lies on the north-east of the island, not far from its northern tip.

Until quite recently visitors to Kenya rarely went further north than Lamu along the coast. Now there are two places for visitors to stay where full facilities are available. One is Kiwaiyu Island Lodge, on the island of Kiwaiyu, north-east of Pate. Access to it is in effect by air only. On the mainland opposite is Kiwaiyu Safari Village, another example of Italian enterprise. It is situated on Mkokoni Bay, 65 km (40 miles) to the north of Lamu. Again access is normally by air. From the village it is possible to visit the Kiunga Marine National Reserve along the coast, and the Dodori National Reserve inland. The Boni National Reserve is further north along the Somali border.

Places to stay

Mombasa

Castle Hotel
Manor Hotel
New Carlton Hotel
Oceanic Hotel
Outrigger Hotel

South Coast

Africana Sea Lodge
Diani Sea Lodge
Diani Reef Hotel
Golden Beach Hotel
Jadini Hotel
Leisure Lodge
Leopard Beach Hotel
Nomad Beach Tented Hotel
Robinson Baobab Hotel
Shelly Beach Hotel
Tradewinds Hotel
Twiga Lodge (cottages)
Two Fishes Hotel

North Coast—Nyali

Mombasa Beach Hotel
Mombasa Beach Apartments
Nyali Beach Hotel
Reef Hotel

North Coast—Bamburi

Bamburi Beach Hotel
Cowrie Shell Apartments
Kenya Beach Hotel
Neptune Beach Hotel
Ocean View Hotel
Plaza Hotel
Severin Sea Lodge
Whitesands Hotel

North Coast—Shanzu

Serena Beach Hotel

North Coast—Kikambala

Sun 'n' Sand Hotel
Whispering Palms Hotel

Kilifi

Sea Horse Hotel

Watamu

Ocean Sports Hotel
Seafarers Hotel
Turtle Bay Hotel

Malindi

Blue Marlin Hotel
Che Shale Club
Driftwood Club
Eden Roc Hotel
Indian Ocean Lodge
Lawford's Hotel
Malindi Chalets
Silversands Beach Cottages
Sindbad Hotel
Suli Suli Club

Tana River

Baomo Lodge

Lamu

New Mahrus Hotel
Peponi Hotel
Petley's Inn

North of Lamu

Kiwaiyu Island Lodge (Kiwaiyu Island)
Kiwaiyu Safari Village (mainland)
Ras Kitau Hotel (Manda Island)

Golf

18-hole course

Nyali Golf Club

9-hole courses

Malindi Golf Club
Mombasa Golf Club

Fishing

Mombasa

Bahari Club
Outrigger Hotel

South Coast—Shimoni

Pemba Channel Fishing Club

North Coast—Mtwapa

Kenya Marinas
F. G. MacConnel and Co.

Kilifi

Sea Horse Hotel

Watamu

Ocean Sports
Seafarers
Turtle Bay Hotel

Malindi

Malindi Sea Fishing Club

Lamu

Peponi Hotel

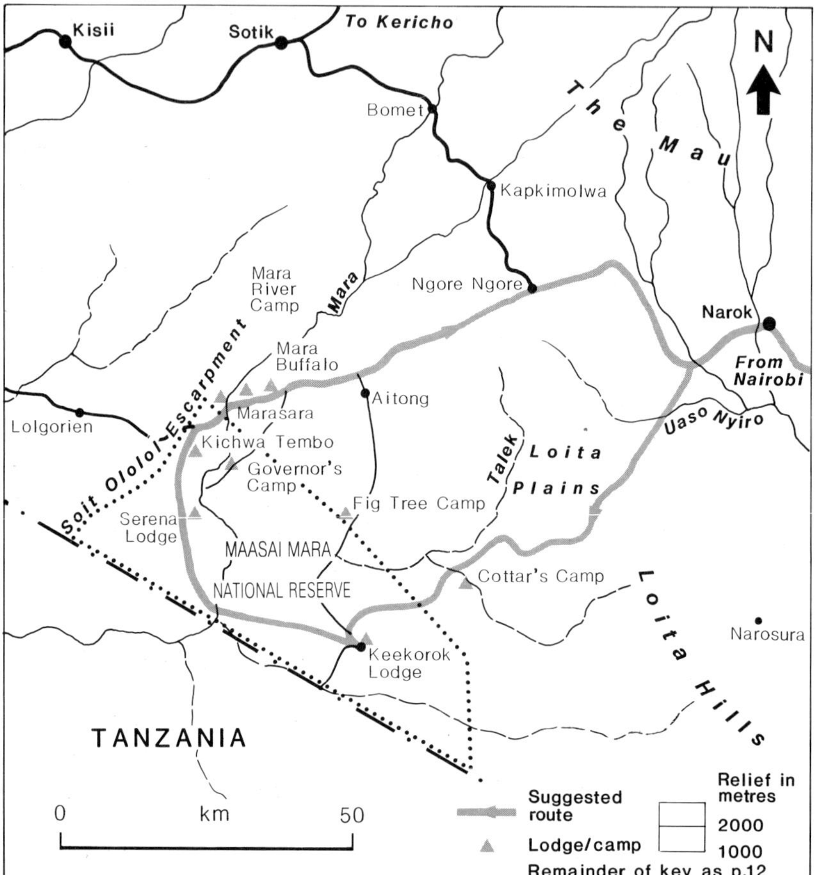

The Mara and Narok

6 The Mara and Maasailand

Maasai Mara National Reserve lies on the Kenya/Tanzania border about 300 km (185 miles) west of Nairobi. It is really a small northern extension of the big Serengeti National Park in Tanzania. The Mara is on the route of the wildebeest migration, when hundreds of thousands of these animals moving periodically in their long columns make their annual circuit of the Serengeti. It takes many weeks, or even months, to pass through any given area, and the dates vary somewhat; in 1981 the migration was at its peak passing through the Mara in the month of August.

Apart from the migration, the Mara has an abundant and varied wildlife that you do not have to travel great distances to see, and the black-maned lions of the area are famous; it is therefore very popular. Even so, the old hunters say that the game of the Mara Triangle is nothing like it was. The Maasai, whose country this is, have of course long since worked out their own *modus vivendi* with game, and if only they and the animals were involved there would not be much cause for anxiety. But poachers from other peoples are a menace here as elsewhere and great inroads have been made by them on the animals, in particular on the rhino and elephant population. The Government has to fight a perennial and difficult war against poaching.

Leave Nairobi by the Uhuru Highway through Westlands. Look out for St Austin's Mission on your left, where some of the earliest coffee was planted, as recorded by Robin Anderson's murals in the Mama Ngina Street Coffee Shop. Climb the hill past Nairobi School to Kabete. If you crossed over the fly-over to the crossroads beyond the Vet. Lab. you would find St Mary's Church on the corner. Straight on and right through the Kabete campus of the university's Faculty of Agriculture would take you to the 9-hole Vet. Lab. golf course. A left turn at St Mary's through the village of Ndumbuini would take you after 2 km (1.25 miles) to a house with stone gate-pillars, in the garden of which are the remains of Fort Smith; only a round hut and a grassy rectangle the size of a small croquet lawn are to be seen, with remnants of walls and a ditch.

Continue through Uthiru, past the Agricultural and Forestry Research Station at Muguga. The road you are on was actually built at the end of the Second World War but it follows an older track. Various places along this road were fortified villages (*ihingo*) when the Kikuyu were moving into the area and settling in the 1880s; besides the villages at Westlands and Waiyaki's near Fort Smith at Kabete, there were others at Kinoo, Kanjeru and Muguga. The villages were carefully concealed in the forest and had their defences covered with living thorny creepers. Father Bernard of St Austin's Mission, who travelled the area looking for a new mission site about 1900, was told that keeping cocks was forbidden in a fortified village in case their crowing betrayed the location to the Maasai.

After turning left near Limuru you enter the Kikuyu Escarpment Forest and descend the Rift's eastern wall, with good views over the valley to your left. Sclater's Road, the old cart road from Nairobi to the north-west made in the 1890s and named after its engineer, descended earlier, passing the other side of the big bluff on your left. After the picnic site halfway down a turning on the right leads to Kijabe, the big Africa Inland Mission station founded by C. E. Hurlburt in 1901, which has a hospital and a printing press as well as schools on the site. There is an attractive small chapel at the foot of the escarpment, all too often vandalized, that was put up by the Italian prisoners of war who built this road in the 1940s.

Ranchland begins and you cross the treed valley of the Kedong River, flowing here mostly under ground. On this stream the Kedong massacre of 1895 took place, in which a large number of porters, mainly Kikuyu, were killed by Maasai. This was not part of any major war between Kikuyu and Maasai, relations between whom were usually fairly easy apart from raiding which didn't count; and even in times of war the Kikuyu women continued to trade with the Maasai. But the 1890s were a turbulent time, and attacks on caravans were increasing. Both Kikuyu and Maasai were hard pressed, having suffered from the devastating rinderpest cattle scourge of 1889–90 and the subsequent smallpox epidemic and famines; as a result Kikuyu men were taking jobs as porters which earlier they would have despised, so that most of the victims of the Kedong massacre were Kikuyu.

Turn off left after 58 km (36 miles) on the tarmac road marked Narok and proceed across the Rift Valley floor past the Longonot Satellite Station. The route lies between two extinct volcanoes. The first, on the right, is Longonot, still streaked with its lava flows. There is a pleasant walk, up and round the crater rim, the starting-point being reached by a track from Longonot Station up the hill towards Naivasha; but leave someone to guard your car at the parking place since it is notorious for thieves. The second, a little later on your left, is Suswa, whose crater wall has blown out on the south side. There is a somewhat inaccessible raised area inside the crater, presumably part of a volcanic plug, which was visited by members of the Operation Drake expedition in 1980. High up on the mountain are a number of caves, quite extensive, which are the home of myriads of bats. Their guano was exploited commercially until recently. But since the company's vehicles no longer travel the route, the track to Suswa from the Narok road, always bad, has become unspeakable.

A Maasai family

Climb the Rift's western wall, still passing scattered groups of Maasai and their cattle herds and an occasional abandoned huddle of huts with a thorn fence round it. Trees increase as you near Narok. There is some cultivation to be seen, and an occasional trading centre with a few *dukas* (native shops). 90 km (56 miles) after turning off at Kijabe you reach Narok, and if there happens to be a dance or celebration planned for the evening you will see a lot of freshly-ochred *moran* in town—a splendid sight. It is one that makes many visitors reach for their cameras, but the impulse must be resisted. The drivers of tour minibuses are instructed to tell their clients bluntly 'DO NOT PHOTOGRAPH THE MAASAI'. Why this ban? Primarily because, as one man put it in a letter to the paper, 'We do not wish to be treated like chimpanzees'. Maasai dress is normal, what you might wear if you were a nomad, not a form of dressing up.

Sensible drivers top up their tanks in Narok in case petrol may be short in the Mara. Their passengers often have a quiet Coke under the umbrellas of the café next to the filling station. This may be a suitable point for a brief digression about the Maasai.

The Maasai think of themselves as being all the Maa-speakers, i.e. everyone who speaks the Maasai languages. Ancestors of the modern Maasai probably moved from around Lake Turkana about AD 1700 to the northern edge of the highlands, then gradually took possession of the grasslands. They are far from being a single homogeneous people. Their main traditional division is between

Maasai watering cattle

the pastoral Rift Valley Maasai who now surround you and the less purely pastoral Wakwavi. The latter include people like the Njemps of Baringo who catch fish; the Samburu, who eat game meat and occasionally cultivate and keep camels; and the Arusha people down in Tanzania who are farmers. The people who created havoc in the coast hinterland in the first half of the 19th century were Wakwavi, 'the dreadful Wakwafi' as Krapf called them, who terrorized the agricultural Chagga and Taita and Kamba peoples. This particular menace seems to have been averted about 1850 by the pastoral Maasai, who defeated and almost exterminated them.

The pastoral Maasai were less bloodthirsty and hostile to their neighbours, but the reputation for extreme aggressiveness seems to have been transferred to them even though their power was waning in the later 19th century. This confusion appears to have been fostered by Arab and Swahili traders in slaves and ivory, who magnified the menace in order to keep curious people away from their business operations.

All sections of the pastoral Maasai are semi-nomadic; that is to say they build houses for themselves and enclosures for their livestock, normally surrounded by a thorn fence. But because of seasonal shortages of water and grazing they do not live in these *enkangs* all the time. Instead, they move on a rough annual circuit determined by the weather.

It is an interesting thought that, here in Narok, you have all the main East

African ways of life, fishing excepted, still going on within a few kilometres of you. Narok itself, with its schools and hospital and club, shops and garages, can stand, with some stretch of the imagination, for modern urban existence. All round it pastoralism continues. Agriculture is represented by the patches of cultivation you have passed, mostly the work of Kikuyu wives married to Maasai, and the big wheat and barley growing scheme on the lower slopes of the Mau. Still further north, higher up in the Mau forests, live a few thousand Wandorobo, hunting, gathering roots and berries and edible vegetation, and collecting honey from their hives.

Leave Narok by the road to the south-west. After 16 km (10 miles) you cross the Uaso Nyiro River (not to be confused with the river of the same name in Laikipia), signing the record book at the police post. Soon after the crossing the road divides. A sharp left turn here would take you through Narosura to the Loita Hills and the top of the Nguruman Escarpment, areas of great natural beauty that are little visited, and on to the Tanzanian border. Of the two roads ahead either will take you to the Mara.

The left fork is the one you choose for the Olemolepo Gate to the game reserve and Keekorok Lodge. The road is usually rough, and leads in a south-westerly direction through open bush across the Loita Plains. 89 km (55 miles) from Narok is Cottar's Camp, for which you turn left at the blue rocks 8 km (5 miles) before the entrance to the reserve. Cottar's is a small and comfortable camp situated on a clear spring among crotons and fig-trees. It is popular with those who like walking through game country; since it is outside the reserve, where you have to stay in your car, movement on foot is possible and a Maasai guide goes with you to ensure safety.

Once inside the game reserve you will be unlucky if you do not see a great variety of animal and bird life. The lions are particularly good; there are big herds of buffalo; the plains game include waterbuck, Tommy (Thomson's gazelle), Grant (Grant's gazelle), eland, lesser kudu, bushbuck and topi, which are very numerous; there are still rhino, as well as elephant and leopard; there are Maasai giraffe; the zebra are Burchell's. Hippo and crocodile can be seen at the right places on the Mara River.

Keekorok is the oldest lodge, solid and comfortable, but there are several other places to stay, each with its own merits. Sarova Mara Camp is 2 km from the main gate. Fig Tree Camp is on the north bank of the Talek River, about 20 km (12.5 miles) north of Keekorok, but outside the reserve. It is usually approached from the more northerly Narok/Mara road, down through Aitong and then turn right before the Talek Gate. The tented camp is about 5 km (3 miles) from that gate.

The road to the west from Keekorok takes you to a bridge over the Mara River quite close to the Tanzanian border and then northwards. About halfway to the northern tip of the reserve from the bridge a road to your right leads to

Giraffe trotting

Mara Serena Lodge, well situated close to the river. Continuing northwards you come to Kichwa Tembo (Elephant Head) Camp on your right, shortly before the reserve boundary. The left turn up the escarpment would take you to Lolgorien and through Kihancha to Migori.

You are out of the reserve by the time you reach the Mara Bridge and the more northerly road back to Narok. Just before the bridge there is a track to the left which follows the west bank of the river and leads to Marasara Camp. Also along this track are the self-help Mara Cottages.

Mara River Camp and Mara Buffalo Camp are across the river on the east bank, also outside the reserve boundary, so that walking is possible. Cross the Mara Bridge and go a few kilometres east towards Narok. The tracks on your left are adequately signposted, if the elephants have not interfered. Some of these tented camps outside the parks—Mara Buffalo is an example—are on the sites of former camps of professional hunters, who used to bring clients to the hunting blocks which they leased. After hunting was made illegal in Kenya in the 1970s as part of the Government's conservation efforts, some of the professionals turned their sites over to the tour business to recover part of their investment.

Going further east, the first track of any importance that you come to on your right, probably with an adequate sign if it has been spared, leads south-west to the best known tented camp of them all, Governor's Camp. It is built in an attractive forested area on the east bank of the Mara, several kilometres down stream from the bridge on a site that has been a favourite camping area for decades. There is also a smaller annexe on the west bank to which they punt you across the river. 'Little Governor's' is popular with local residents and particularly good for birds. Governor's Camp is of course inside the game reserve, where the usual rules of conduct apply.

The main road back to the east is another rough and stony route that will rattle your teeth, but the earlier part of it around Aitong, where it runs through low hills, is quite attractive. The only major turning you come to is reached 56 km (35 miles) short of Narok, where a left turn at Ngore Ngore leads to the Maasai boundary at Kapkimolwa and across the Mara into the Kipsigis country around Bomet (the former Sotik Post); from there it is a relatively easy journey to Kericho or Kisii.

This country northwards to Bomet used to be very difficult to traverse in the rains, because though the hills are covered with red soil the valleys are filled with a black cotton soil that becomes very sticky when wet. There was once a District Commissioner, called Clarence Buxton who was concerned to encourage athletics and had a passion for stadia; he built a stadium both at Kisii and at Narok. He was DC Kisii when orders arrived posting him to Narok, and this posed a certain problem since his wife had a grand piano that the haul in a truck might damage. So he decided to employ porters to move it.

Unfortunately the rains broke early that year, while the party carrying the piano was still in southern Kipsigis, and they were unable to negotiate the valleys. They deposited their load on a hilltop and built a thatched roof over it. When they returned in drier weather several months later and completed delivery at Narok the piano only needed tuning.

Your road continues round the northern edge of the Loita Plains through open bush country. As you draw nearer to the Uaso Nyiro, you begin to see on your left extensive fields of wheat. Just before you cross the river, 16 km (10 miles) short of Narok, the road from Keekorok joins yours and the circuit is completed.

During the colonial period some officers of the British administration who served in these parts of the country used to become fascinated, almost to the point of obsession, with the pastoral way of life and its independence and self-sufficiency. Cases of Maasai-itis, as it was called, were treated tolerantly by their fellow officers. You are probably in no danger of contracting the disease after such a short exposure. But long after you leave Kenya you will probably recall the sight of a man standing comfortably on one leg and holding a spear, not nagged by material wants, serenely contemplating his wealth, perhaps as much as 200,000 shillings' worth of it, on the hoof.

Places to stay

Cottar's Camp
Fig Tree Camp
Governor's Camp
Keekorok Lodge
Kichwa Tembo Camp
Mara Buffalo Camp
Mara Cottages (self-help)
Mara River Camp
Marasara Camp
Mara Serena Lodge
Sarova Mara Camp

Golf

Kabete
9-hole course
Vet. Lab. Golf Club

Western Kenya

7 Western Kenya

A circuit west of the Rift Valley can provide more variety of scenery among more diverse peoples than any other Kenya safari. Most of this country has only one long rainy season, from the beginning of April to about September, and if you hit a wet spell during that half of the year you may have to stay on main roads and not venture far off tarmac. If you wait till March the Lake Victoria basin can be uncomfortably hot during the day. October and November are good months for a visit, especially since the flowering trees and plants are then at their best; long stretches of the roads in Luhya country and Kipsigis are lined with colour, particularly yellow—*cassias*, members of the daisy family, the flower of the Mauritius thorn used for marking boundaries, and many others.

Pack carefully. Anti-malarial tablets are necessary for the Lake area, as really for most parts of Kenya under 1500 metres (5000 feet). You need warm clothing for the western highlands in the evenings, and light clothes, a hat and sunglasses for daytime Kisumu. A raincoat or plastic mac could be useful, since afternoon or evening storms are quite common round the lake even in the dry season, sometimes with cracking thunder and teeming rain. But mornings in western Kenya are almost always bright and sparkling, and mud roads that have been soaked the night before dry quickly in the sun.

The western highlands are the home of the Kalenjin, a group of nine or more peoples speaking mutually intelligible Southern Nilotic languages. *Kalenjin* means 'I tell you', and is a convenient name coined in modern times for the group. They include the Kipsigis, the Nandi, the Teriki, the Elgeyo and Marakwet, the Tugen, the Pokot, the Kony, whom people used to call 'Elgon Maasai', and the Sebei, the majority of whom live across in Uganda. The Dorobo forest-dwellers on the Mau speak a Nandi-type language, presumably from long association with the Kalenjin, and are often included as another Kalenjin group, the Okiek. The open grasslands of the western highlands, once dominated by the Maasai and used by them for seasonal grazing, were settled by Europeans in the colonial period, and the Nairobi/Kitale road was a main White Highlands artery.

In the country of medium altitude to the west of the Kalenjin are Kenya's western Bantu peoples, the Abaluhya and their neighbours to the south, whose homelands extend from the foothills of Elgon down through the southern part of the western highlands to the Tanzanian border. Beyond and further west again, round the lake shore, live the Luo, Western Nilotes who are the most southerly of the Lwoo-speaking peoples. They are Kenya's third most numerous group after the Kikuyu and the Abaluhya.

Nairobi to Nakuru

Take the main road to the north out of Nairobi as described in Chapter 2 for visiting Lake Naivasha. After you cross the Malewa River you drive through an undulating landscape along the bed of the Rift. This high part of the Rift floor from Lake Naivasha to Nakuru and beyond includes some of Kenya's best ranching country. Steers from less favoured regions are brought to farms in the Gilgil area to be fattened for the market.

Gilgil itself is a small garrison town with a camp of the National Youth Service, a club with a 9-hole golf course, and an old-established boys' preparatory school called Pembroke House. At the foot of the slope beyond the township is Lake Elmenteita, a soda lake valuable only to flamingoes, who come here periodically. Beyond the lake, to the west, is Lord Delamere's ranch, Soysambu. There is a curiously-shaped hill here which looks like a man lying on his back, and in some lights the features bear a certain resemblance to those of that Hugh Cholmondeley, third Baron Delamere, who was Kenya's most famous European settler.

As you drive into Nakuru, 64 km (40 miles) from Naivasha, you can appreciate what a cardinal position the town occupies and how it became the farming capital of the highlands. The narrow passage between Lake Nakuru to the south and the big caldera of Menengai to the north is a convenient route for both main road and railway to cross the Rift Valley to where its western wall can be climbed.

At 1800 metres (6000 feet) Nakuru is a pleasant place, except in those rare dry periods when the wind blows soda over the town from the lake. It is an industrial and commercial centre, with flour mills, a Union Carbide plant, a blanket factory, a training school where the Forest Department makes prefabricated wooden houses for its forest stations, and many other industries. The Kenya Farmers' Association, the country's oldest agricultural co-operative, has its main establishment here, and so does the pyrethrum industry. A powerful natural insecticide is made from the dried flowers of the pyrethrum daisy, much in demand by those who prefer to avoid chemical pesticides.

The main attraction for visitors is the Lake Nakuru National Park, only a few kilometres south of the town, which is one of the world's great bird sanctuaries. Many hundreds of thousands of flamingoes live in the Rift Valley, moving up and down it between Ethiopia and northern Tanzania, where Lake Natron is their chief breeding-place. The algae which thrive in the Rift's soda lakes are their favourite food, and they have a filter mechanism in their mouths which allows them to swallow the algae and reject the water.

The park has been extended in recent years by the inclusion of the old Long and Hopcraft farms, hides have been built, and roads improved; it is possible to drive right round the lake except when the water level is high. There is accommodation at Lake Nakuru Lodge and Lion Hill Camp.

Two other short excursions from Nakuru are worth making. One is to Hyrax Hill, 5 km (3 miles) out of town to the north of the Nairobi road, which is an archaeological site of interest. It has remains of several periods, including a New Stone Age settlement dated to about 1000 BC and an Iron Age settlement of relatively recent date which consists of round structures roughly built with stone. There is a museum on the site in the former home of Mrs Mary Selfe; she gave her house as a memorial to her son, an airman who died in the Second World War.

There is also a track leading from the higher part of the town up past Nakuru School to a look-out point on the rim of the Menengai Crater, from where the view is superb. Be careful if you descend into the caldera itself; the going is very rough, and puff adders are common.

As for accommodation in Nakuru, the two main hotels are the Stag's Head and the Midland, only a block apart in the middle of town. Nakuru golf course, 18 holes round the lower slopes of Menengai, is beautiful but not easy.

Nakuru to Eldoret

Leave Nakuru by the main road to the west, up the long hill past Nakuru Junction, where the branch line to Kisumu leaves the main line to Eldoret and Uganda. Notice on your left 12 km (7.5 miles) out of town the sign 'A.D.C. Ngata Complex', where the Agricultural Development Corporation manages what was formerly one of President Kenyatta's farms. In colonial times Ngata Farm belonged to Lord Egerton of Tatton, a reputed misogynist and music lover who built himself a substantial castle on the estate. The castle's hall was furnished with a fully piped organ on which the owner used to play by the hour the classical repertoire from pianola-type rolls. His name is commemorated by Egerton College at Njoro, a little way to the south-west. This is the Government's main agricultural training institution, for which he gave the land.

The road runs straight for several kilometres across the Rift floor through sizeable fields. There is a lot of wheat, some sunflower and cattle, mainly Friesians. The hill ahead of you is Mount Londiani, 3008 metres (9872 feet). The Rift wall is continued to the left by the long line of the Mau Escarpment. Away to your right, north of Mount Londiani, are Eldama Ravine and Tugen country beyond.

Pelicans and flamingoes on Lake Nakuru

As you climb the far side of the Rift the vegetation changes. The big euphorbia candelabra soon give way to bigger acacias and erythrinas; as you near the old Jolly Farmer Hotel, now used by the Kenya Police, patches of cedar and olive forest begin to appear; then come coniferous plantations of the Forest Department before the turn-off to Molo 45 km (28 miles) from Nakuru; and finally there are grassy downs with many sheep until you reach the turn-off to Kericho and Kisumu 54 km (33 miles) from Nakuru at an altitude of 2559 metres (8400 feet). Notice all the tin roofs glinting in the sun on your right; these are usually the sign of a co-operative settlement scheme. Many former European farms were bought after Independence by groups of African farmers. One common pattern was for the new settlers to form a co-operative, retain small plots for themselves and their families, and employ a skilled manager to run the major part of the holding.

Go straight on towards Eldoret past Mount Londiani. There are wide views on your left towards the Tinderet Forest. 69 km (42 miles) from Nakuru you pass through the trading centre of Makutano where a right turn leads to Eldama Ravine, a place once better known than it is now. There was a Government station there on the route to Uganda in the 1890s and in 1897 some Sudanese troops, the rump of the force commanded by Emin Pasha in the southern Sudan, mutinied and set off for home; they were checked only after a sharp engagement in what is now Western Province. Later that same year Delamere, arriving from a shooting expedition in Somalia, climbed up from

Lake Baringo and entered the Kenya highlands for the first time at Ravine. His party's arrival caused some dismay to the Maltese Collector in charge of the station, James Martin, who had received a garbled warning of an armed invasion from Ethiopia.

The road through Eldama Ravine from the Nakuru/Baringo road, by the way, is worth considering as an alternative route from Nakuru to Makutano. It is at present in better condition than the main road, but is 14 km (9 miles) longer.

The road continues to climb, crossing the Equator 86 km (53 miles) from Nakuru. The 2742 metre (9000 foot) railway station at Timboroa is claimed to be the highest in the Commonwealth. The long descent passes through forest reserve—conifer plantations and fields of wheat, the residents on the settlement schemes being mainly Kikuyu and Nandi—past the turn-off to Nandi Hills after 109.5 km (58 miles), through Tarakwa (the Burnt Forest of old), and out on to the Uasin Gishu plateau after about 133 km (82 miles).

At the end of the 19th century all this country was virtually uninhabited except by game. The Uasin Gishu Maasai, dominant before 1850, had first been harried by the Nandi, then almost destroyed in wars against other Maasai groups, and the remnants had gone; Joseph Thomson, on his journey for the Royal Geographical Society, met a few of them in 1883 living in Kabras. Such Kalenjin herds as moved back to graze the plateau had been decimated by the

The Kerio Valley from the Kapchebelel Escarpment

rinderpest epidemic of 1889–90. So it is not surprising that Uasin Gishu was seen in the 1900s first as a hunter's paradise and then as land ripe for settlement. The late Cecil Hoey, who lived for many years on the Cheranganis, describes in his memoirs how he used to spend the day on Sergoit Rock (the hill to the north-east of Eldoret) 'with my glasses, watching the vast herds of game below me'. He actually watched from the rock the arrival through the forest of the ox wagons of the Van Rensburg trek in 1908–09, the last of the historic Afrikaner treks.

The appearance of big plantations of black wattle along the road tells you that you are nearing Eldoret. Wattle-bark contains tannin, and a tannin extract factory is one of Eldoret's industries. The town itself is of some size, with well-treed suburbs, a university, many churches and schools, and a club with a 9-hole golf course crossing the Sosiani River. The centre of town still has many buildings that recall Cape Dutch and wide streets originally designed for spans of oxen to turn in. The newest hotel is the Sirikwa. The older ones are the Highlands Inn, New Lincoln and New Wagon Wheel.

However, you may prefer to stay out of town. If so, there are two country pubs worth consideration. One is the Kaptagat Hotel, altitude 2376 metres (7800 feet), 34 km (21 miles) out to the south-east along the tarmac road to the Kapchebelel Escarpment, from which a gravel road was built down to a fluorspar mine in the Kerio Valley through spectacular scenery. Trout fishing is available from the hotel. Not much more than a kilometre away, along the banks of the Ellegirini River, is a group of about ten 'Sirikwa holes'. They are all in people's private gardens, but the hotel is sometimes able to help with a visit. Sirikwa holes are circular stone-lined pits, 4 or 5 metres in diameter but sometimes larger, found in hundreds over much of the Plateau and Trans Nzoia and down into the Rift. They are from 200 to 500 years old. Local tradition attributes them to an earlier population called the Sirikwa. They were in fact almost certainly built as defensible cattle-pens by earlier Kalenjin-speaking groups, presumably the ancestors of the present inhabitants. They seem to have given up building them when the pens proved no safeguard against Maasai incursions into the grasslands. Houses are sometimes found in association with Sirikwa holes; there is an example down at Tambach where the associated house is built of stone. The round stone-lined pits which you may have seen at Hyrax Hill are Sirikwa holes also.

26 km (16 miles) north-west of Eldoret, on the road to Kitale, is Soy Country Club, membership of which is open to visitors. It is a small country hotel built in the form of a courtyard round a pond. There is a somewhat sporting 9-hole golf course outside the sitting-room. The hotel may be able to help you to fish the Moiben River near by, but the fishing is said to have suffered from poaching.

Nandi country can easily be visited from Eldoret. Its administrative centre is

Kapsabet, 48 km (30 miles) to the south. If you think the cattle look rather better than usual, spare a thought for Warwick Guy, who elected to spend 25 years for this purpose at the Baraton Veterinary Station just up the road from Kapsabet.

Another objective for a visit is Kamarin, 34 km (21 miles) from Eldoret, an agricultural showground on the edge of the Elgeyo Escarpment with a great view across the Rift over the Tugen Hills towards Mount Kenya. To get there you leave Eldoret on the Sergoit road to the north-east and turn right to Iten; Kamarin is just beyond. From here a road winds down the escarpment to Kessup AIC (African Inland Church) mission and Tambach.

You can make a longer and rougher trip to the Rift edge by following the road past Sergoit Rock to Cheblemit and down through the candelabra forest to Kapsowar in Marakwet with its mission hospital. North of this is the infamous Tot Escarpment, beloved of the organizers of the Marlboro Safari Rally, held annually at Easter. Along this escarpment are kilometres of irrigation furrows, still in use, thought to be the product of earlier Kalenjin enterprise.

Eldoret to Kitale

Leave town on the main road to Uganda, turn right after 14 km (9 miles) on to the road past Soy, pass the Loreto Convent at Matunda, and you reach the end of the Plateau at Moi's Bridge (formerly Hoey's Bridge), 60 km (37 miles) from Eldoret.

On crossing the bridge over the Nzoia River you enter gently rolling country, warm enough for thorn trees, with pastures, sunflower and, above all, maize. This area east of Mount Elgon, together with the Bungoma area south of the mountain, is Kenya's chief granary, maize being still the staple food of the majority of the population. Growing maize likes to be quite warm at night as well as during the day, and the country round Elgon meets this requirement.

The main township is Kitale, 1913 metres (6280 feet), which is railhead, 69 km (43 miles) from Eldoret. You enter past the National Agricultural Research Station and Kitale Club, which has a fine 18-hole golf course. The Kitale Hotel is right in the middle of the township. It can supply information on local fishing facilities.

Apart from a colourful market, the chief place of interest is the National Museum of Western Kenya founded by Lt-Col C. T. Stoneham. Stoneham himself was a bird and butterfly enthusiast, but the display in the museum concentrates on the artifacts of the peoples round about—Turkana, Abaluhya, Marakwet and Pokot.

There are two National Parks in the area, the Saiwa Swamp and Mount Elgon. To reach the first you leave Kitale by the Kapenguria road, which is clearly signposted. You cross the Saiwa River 19 km from Kitale and the turning to the park is immediately on your right. The swamp is the home of the *sitatunga*, a water antelope rather like a taller bushbuck with markedly spiral horns. It has broad elongated hooves which allow it to walk on boggy ground. It is very rare in Kenya, being found only here and in papyrus swamps round Lake Victoria.

If you go further out along the main road towards Pokot country you come to Kapenguria, 32 km (20 miles) from Kitale, where Mzee Jomo Kenyatta stood trial during the Mau Mau Emergency for managing an unlawful society. A hard-surface road is now being built from here to Lodwar, which will make Turkana more accessible than it has so far been.

If you want to fish the Cherangani trout streams you should contact the Kapolet Fishing Association, PO Box 332, Kitale, who have a small fishing camp on the Kapolet River about 22 km (14 miles) north-east of Kitale. The best fishing is reported to be on the Morun, high up on the Cheranganis, where there are good brown trout in the upper reaches, rainbow below them, and barbel lower still. However, this involves a 4-wheel drive journey up the Cherangani Highway, the track that runs along the spine of the Cheranganis from Kapenguria to Iten, and a very chilly night of camping out at about 2742 metres (9000 feet), since there is no accommodation.

To reach Mount Elgon National Park you leave Kitale to the west. If there is rain about, ignore the first sign to the park on your left and take the second access road from Endebess at the end of the tarmac 17 km (10.5 miles) out of town. Notice the stands of maize along this road, and the establishments of the Kenya Seed Company, a successful local enterprise that farmers look to for their hybrid maize seed. From Endebess take the Saboti road past Elgon Downs Farm and follow the signs up into the foothills. Mount Elgon Lodge is about 14 km (9 miles) up the dirt road and the park gate not far beyond it.

The lodge is at 2163 metres (7100 feet) under the bluff on Elgon. It is in fact the spacious old Howard de Walden house, with a line of five double cottages built out at the back. It must be one of the finest house sites in the country, with Trans Nzoia before you and the mountain behind. A family or small group might prefer to stay at the guest house on the Mills' Lokitela Farm, which is in the same general area but lower down, 19 km (11 miles) west of Kitale. (Mr and Mrs A.C. Mills, PO Box 122, Kitale.)

The park itself is a forest park, which means that its tracks are likely to be impassable in the rains. But when movement is possible there is some fine forest and its game to see, and some good mountain walking on the moorland higher up. Elgon is a big mountain, covering about 2589 sq km (1000 square miles), and rising to 4321 metres (14 181 feet). The summit consists of a string of rocky peaks round a crater. There are hot springs near the top, and the area is dotted with caves, most of them natural but some excavated or extended by man. Several contain rock paintings.

Kitale to Kisumu

Drive out of Kitale on the Nairobi road and turn right at the agricultural research station on the outskirts of the township. The road leads past the airfield and through Kiminini. Soon after the turning to your left marked Turbo you leave what used to be White Highlands and enter the country of the Abaluhya peoples, in this case the Bukusu. Notice how the old round thatched huts with the central pole sticking out are giving way to rectangular thatched houses.

The tarmac turning to the right at Kamakoiwa leads to Kimilili and, 2 km (1.25 miles) of dirt road beyond it, Friends' School, Kamusinga. Kamusinga, a boys' secondary school established since the Second World War with help from English Quakers, stands near the northern boundary of one of the old mission empires. American Quaker mission work started in Luhya country as early as 1902, and the main station at Kaimosi, south of Kakamega, is still an important religious and educational centre. Quakerism won such a following among the Abaluhya that the Yearly Meeting here became the largest in the world and had to be divided up.

Kimilili is the home of Elijah Masinde, a remarkable figure in Kenya's recent history. An international footballer, he became a flamboyant nationalist and leader of *Dini ya Msambwa*, one of the country's many independent religious

S.S. Victoria at Kisumu pier

sects. Most of these sects are law-abiding, but *Dini ya Msambwa* was not. It caused much trouble to the colonial administration, including the Kolloa Affray of 1950 in which about 30 people were killed down in the Kerio Valley. This led to its being proscribed. Freedom to operate after Independence was again abused, and the Republic finally banned the sect in 1968.

Return to the main road at Misikhu trading centre. The next place of importance is Lugulu, at the edge of the high ground before the Nzoia River valley. Lugulu is the northern centre for the Friends' Africa Mission, with a mission hospital and a girls' high school. It is also the site of a battle which the Bukusu fought against the British in 1895. The Bukusu had been amassing stolen British weapons, and the askaris (African soldiers) sent to get them back were murdered; so C. W. Hobley, the first Nyanza Provincial Commissioner, led a force from his Mumias headquarters to the scene. The stockaded village at Lugulu was besieged and captured, but only at the cost of hand-to-hand fighting and many casualties.

Go down the hill to the main Uganda road and turn left into Webuye (formerly Broderick Falls), with its Pan African Paper Mill. Having crossed the river beyond the township take the right-hand turn-off to Kakamega. This stretch of road runs through Kabras, the Kabras people being another section of the Abaluhya. When Joseph Thomson visited them in 1883 he found them prosperous and able to provide ample supplies for his men. 'We were in the midst of abundance', he wrote. His book, *Through Masailand*, contains an engraving of a Kabras village surrounded by its mud wall and dry ditch, which it was the custom to build at the time.

The long line of the Nandi Escarpment on your left is the western boundary of Nandi country. Between the escarpment and the road, as it nears Kakamega, is the Kakamega Forest, of interest to biologists since it contains plant and animal species not commonly found elsewhere in Kenya. 51 km (31 miles) from Webuye you reach Kakamega town, headquarters of Western Province.

The township has the modern Kakamega Golf Hotel, the older Highway Hotel, and a club with a challenging 9-hole golf course. During the Idi Amin era in Uganda there was a big camp for Ugandan refugees in the township. In the 1930s gold was found in the area by an American, L. A. Johnson, and there was a minor gold rush of European farmers who temporarily abandoned their farms during the slump and came to the Kakamega goldfield in hope of better things. Few made a fortune, because the sub-surface strata are too churned up to allow for consistent production. But many amateur miners made enough to tide them over the bad times. Small amounts of gold are still found by local people panning in the streams round about.

Leaving Kakamega via Mukumu on the Kisumu road you cross the Yala River and reach Chavakali at the top of the hill beyond, where a turning to the left leads to Kaimosi and Teriki country. The Teriki are a small Kalenjin-speaking group whose homeland forms a salient from south of Nandi out to the west.

From Chavakali through Mbale to Vihiga you are in Maragoli, which is the most densely populated rural area in Kenya. The turn-off to your left marked Serem leads to a winding road along the top of the Nyando Escarpment which reaches Kaptumo, site of one of the forts built to check Nandi attacks on the railway line at the turn of the century, and finally the tea-growing district of Nandi Hills. After the Nyangori Mission the road runs downhill. Look left as you descend and note the tall pinnacle known as the Nandi Rock, from which malefactors are supposed to have been thrown to execution. At the foot of the long hill is Kisumu.

Kisumu

The Winam (formerly Kavirondo) Gulf, together with the low-lying Kano Plains, divide western Kenya into two parts, and the link between the two is Kisumu, headquarters of Nyanza Province. The altitude of Lake Victoria is 1133 metres (3718 feet), so the town is a warm and relaxed sort of place, tending to be humid in February and March. It is a natural centre for visiting the western areas of the country.

Like Nairobi, Kisumu is a modern town dating from the turn of the century and owing its existence to the railway. The terminus decided upon for the Uganda Railway was Port Florence, and from there the link to Uganda was to be by ship across the lake. The site of Port Florence was Old Kisumu, round the other side of Ogowe Bay from the modern town, where the airfield and industrial estate and 9-hole golf course are now. When the engineers eventually built the port on the south side of the bay Hobley, the PC (Provincial Commissioner), decided to move the growing township to the ridge above the station, which was a healthier site.

The chief hotel is the Sunset, opened in 1977, 1.3 km (0.8 mile) southwards towards the Yacht Club and the recreation area of Hippo Point. It has a good view out over the lake. In the middle of town is the New Kisumu Hotel, a big structure built after the last war to provide for passengers on the flying boats which at that time landed at Kisumu; it has no air-conditioning, but all the windows outside the bedrooms are covered with wire mesh, so that the building is like a giant meat-safe and free of most insects.

Kisumu is good for birds, and many species—herons and egrets, ibis, storks, fish eagles and cormorants—can be seen along the lake shore without leaving the township. The rough ground along the lake between the two main hotels is inhabited by a small municipal herd of semi-tame impala. On the edge of town, out on the Nairobi road, is the Kisumu Museum opened in 1980. It is a good example of a local museum, showing the traditional occupations of the peoples round about, their weapons, games, musical instruments and medicines. Even the snakes are local—a black mamba from Chemelil, for example, and a forest cobra found near the municipal sewage. There is a model of a Luo homestead outside, at the back.

Kisumu to Port Victoria

Various trips can be made from Kisumu to the country between the town and Uganda. The main tarmac road to Busia, 130 km (81 miles) from Kisumu, passes through the border area between the Luo and Luhya peoples. They are quite mixed up here, but as far as the Nzoia River those living to the left of the road are mainly Luo and those to the right mainly Luhya.

The first main road to the left after you leave the Winam Gulf behind leads to Bondo. North of where this road reaches the lake is Ramogi Hill, an important place in Luo history. Named after a mythical ancestor, it is a defensible area where some of the early Luo immigrants settled after moving to Kenya from the north. On Ramogi Hill, says the historian B. A. Ogot, this semi-nomadic group took the first major step in the 'transition to the life of an agricultural people'.

25 km (15 miles) from Kisumu you reach Maseno, an old Church Missionary Society station dating from the beginning of the century. There are a teachers' college, now Government-run, a secondary school and a hospital.

7 km (4 miles) on you reach Luanda, from which a tarmac road to the left leads to Siaya, the district centre. The last village before Siaya is Ng'iya, where the CMS once ran a primary teachers' college, now a girls' high school. The old college buildings and the charming St John's Church are still in being.

There is a crossroads 75 km (46 miles) from Kisumu, where a left turn will take you across the Nzoia River to the pleasant shady township of Ukwala. Turn left again, and you will come eventually to the lake at Port Victoria. The township, which has a wide square with a market under the trees, and canned music coming from the *dukas*, is reminiscent of the eastern Mediterranean. There is no port—it is a fishing village only, with canoes drawn up on the grass. The Mulukoba Lakeside Hotel at the water's edge has accommodation and offers a warm welcome. John Osogo, after whom the secondary school is named, was a distinguished historian from a local family who died in 1979; his younger brother James served as a Minister in the cabinets of President Kenyatta and President Moi.

Port Victoria was once intended to be the Lake Victoria terminus of the Uganda Railway. Then a second survey in 1895–6 under Blackett found a way through the hills further south and down on to the Kano Plains which saved 120 km (75 miles) of railway, and Kisumu was finally chosen. Even so, Port Victoria continued to have a British garrison during the 1890s and the hydrographic survey of northern Lake Victoria was carried out from here in

The market at Bungoma

1898–9. The surveyor concerned, Lt B. Whitehouse R.N., was the brother of the railway's chief engineer.

As you retrace your steps from Port Victoria, take the first turning to the left leading to Sio Port. This is all Luhya country again, and Port Victoria and Sio Port are twin fishing villages. The map marks a jetty at Sio Port, but no ships call. If a jetty still exists it is buried deep in a thicket of papyrus 4.5 metres (15 feet) high which masks the lake from the foreshore. Through the papyrus has been cut a channel perhaps 60 metres (65 yards) long to the lake, and this secluded tunnel was one of the main routes by which Uganda coffee was smuggled into Kenya during the Idi Amin years. From Sio Port a wider dirt road takes you back through Nangina to join the Busia/Kisumu tarmac at Bumala, a bustling market.

Kisumu to Bungoma

Set out again on the Busia road but take the right turn to Mumias after 37 km (23 miles). There is a stretch of about 40 km (25 miles) of gravel road, normally in fair condition, before you reach tarmac again near Mumias. This township is the capital of the old kingdom of Wanga, one of the smaller kingdoms in what was eastern Uganda until 1902. The dynasty of the Wanga ruling family has lasted several hundred years and there is a remembered history of eighteen kings, called Nabongos. The capital was established at what is now Mumias at the end of the 18th century. Mumia himself was Nabongo when Joseph Thomson came in 1883, and Hobley made his first headquarters nearby in the next decade. Although the British abolished most of the political powers of the kingdom in the 1920s on Mumia's death, the line still goes on. The present Nabongo's duties are mainly ritual. His office is near that of the District Officer, by the big eucalyptus trees out on the old Kisumu road. There are two market days each week in the township, and the market dues are paid on one day to the Government and on the other to the Nabongo. The modern prosperity of Mumias depends on its sugar factory.

27 km (17 miles) north of Mumias is Bungoma, on the main railway line. It is the principal collecting centre for the maize grown south of Mount Elgon, the chief Bukusu administrative centre, and a fast-growing town. The Bungoma Tourist Hotel, a project of the Kenya National Union of Teachers, is on the Mumias road. If you take the right-hand turn-off marked Kakamaga about 5 km (3 miles) short of Bungoma you reach, past the tree nursery at Sangalo, a village called Mwibale with a prominent rocky outcrop, also called Mwibale, just to the north. This hill is worth climbing. There is a large water storage tank on it built in 1955, and by means of an ingenious series of concrete walls and channels much of the rain falling on the hill is stored, then used to irrigate the *shambas* below. Near the top are what look like footprints in the solid rock, known to the local people as 'Footsteps of Mulia', a semi-mythical ancestor.

4 km (2.5 miles) north of Bungoma is the main Uganda road. A left turn would bring you to the border at Malaba after 32 km (20 miles). But before you reached it you would cross a less defined boundary—the Bantu Line. That is to say, from here, virtually no Bantu speakers live between you and Cairo, but most of the Africans between you and Cape Town are Bantu-speaking. You have just come through Bukusu country, but along the international boundary live the Iteso, an Eastern Nilotic people whose language belongs with those of the Turkana to the north and Maasai away to the south-east. South of the road is Amukura Catholic Mission with its high school; a short distance beyond the mission is the homestead of Flora, sculptor of delicate black clay heads and figures.

If heavy rain threatens you may prefer to do a few extra kilometres via Webuye and Kakamega and have tarmac back to Kisumu.

Kisumu to Kisii and South Nyanza

Leave Kisumu by the Nairobi road across the flat Kano Plains. The wide smiles, dark skins, gracefully carried head loads, euphorbia-encircled homesteads, old ladies smoking pipes—all the signs you are used to by now—will confirm that this is Luo country. Cross the Nyando River at Ahero (km 22), where the National Irrigation Board has been developing rice production, then take the right turn to the south. This is a tarmac road all the way to the Tanzanian border at Isebania.

Cross the plain and climb the slope towards Sondu. Cross the Sondu River, which is the district boundary, and continue towards Oyugis. After the first turn-off to Kendu Bay, the next turning to your left at the police post would take you towards the hills and the Charachani River; here the Kisii, after years of losing cattle to Kipsigis raiders, finally ambushed the Kipsigis army returning from a major raid about 1890 and, reinforced by the Luo, inflicted a heavy defeat. A peace of exhaustion seems to have ensued that lasted until British administration was introduced a few years later.

A right turn at Oyugis leads to Kendu Bay, a small lake port which shares with Homa Bay a scheduled boat service to Kisumu. Continuing south, you would reach Kisii after 34 km (21 miles), but the main Tanzania road turns off to the right a few kilometres short of the town. Further down this road you will notice the Seventh Day Adventist Mission at Kamagambo, 27 km (17 miles) from Kisii. In this area the Gusii people dig out of the hillsides the soapstone which they carve into figures, pots, ashtrays etc. The stone is quite soft when extracted, but hardens later. It is light-coloured, but many of the figures are stained black for sale. Not all Kisii carving is this light-hearted commercial work; there are serious sculptors as well. A stone bird at the entrance to Unesco headquarters in Paris is the work of a Gusii sculptor, Elkana Ong'esa.

Luo fisherman with net, Homa Bay

After Kamagambo you are back in Luo country and come soon to Rongo, where a right turn leads to Homa Bay. The Homa Bay Hotel is comfortable and the most convenient base from which to visit the Lambwe Valley. This small game reserve is the best place in Kenya to see roan antelope. The entrance is only 17 km (10.5 miles) from Homa Bay. Self-help *bandas* have been built just outside the reserve. Beyond the valley the road runs out to Mbita Point, from which boats cross to Rusinga Island, site of some major fossil discoveries by Dr Leakey and birthplace of Tom Mboya, an outstanding politician of the early years of Independence, murdered in Nairobi in 1969.

Beyond Rongo to the south are Awendo, with another sugar factory, and Migori: gold is still panned in the Migori River. A left turn here would take you via Kihancha, with its forest bird sanctuary near by, to Lolgorien and down the escarpment into the Maasai Mara.

If you return to Kisumu up the main road you should visit Kisii, which is an attractive town on a hillside. Kisii Hotel and the Mwalimu Hotel offer accommodation. There is a sporting 9-hole golf course. The town was captured and held for a time by the Germans in the First World War and both German and British soldiers are buried in the graveyard. The Gusii, a Bantu-speaking people, are keen farmers who suffered for years because of their distance from railhead. Nowadays in their highlands, a series of tall conical hills with valleys between, they grow a lot of tea.

Kisumu to Nairobi

For the main route back to Nairobi from Kisumu you drive east from the town across the Kano Plains without turning right at Ahero. The left turn at Awasi, 41 km (26 miles) from Kisumu, leads to the Chemelil Sugar Factory and up the scenic escarpment to Nandi Hills, where there are tea estates. The 9-hole golf course at the club in Nandi Hills is well kept.

Between the two turn-offs to Muhoroni (another sugar factory) 57 km (35 miles) from Kisumu you come to the county boundary and the border country between Luoland and Kipsigis. It is said that friction along this border was once so violent that an early PC (Provincial Commissioner) had a continuous ditch dug, a sort of Offa's Dyke, to keep the peoples apart, but I have never seen any traces. The population gets thinner as you begin the climb back into the highlands, there are belts of scrub and forest, and about 66 km (41 miles) from Kisumu you first see small neatly-hedged fields of Kipsigis pasture and cultivation. There are dozens of these attractive holdings between here and Kericho, with maize, beans, good grass, some bananas, and progressively more stands of tea. The hedges may be *macrocarpa* or Mauritius thorn or just bush plants. This farming pattern is not traditional but dates from colonial times, notably the decade when Cyril Barwell was District Agricultural Officer. The

A tea plucker. The pluckers break off the young shoots carefully and put them in baskets on their backs. After weighing, the leaf is transported to the factory without delay. The leaf is first withered, then rolled and sifted. The rolling starts a process of fermentation, and the tea is laid out on trays in humid conditions until it is ready to be dried. The dried leaf comes out of the driers as black tea, ready to be sorted and packed.

houses are partly rectangular tin with tin roofs and partly traditional circular thatched.

By the time you enter Kericho, district headquarters and seat of the Kipsigis County Council, you have travelled 83 km (52 miles) from Kisumu and climbed from 1140 metres to 1980 metres (3800 feet to 6600 feet). Kericho is a nice small town with most of the central and local government offices on the west side of the main road and a small park on the east side, behind which lie Holy Trinity Church and the DC's house. The Tea Hotel is comfortable, and can provide details of the local fishing available. The Kericho/Sotik Fishing Association, PO Box 281, Kericho, welcomes visiting trout fishermen to its waters and charges modest rates for temporary membership. A map can be bought for Shs. 2/- showing the trout streams issuing from the West Mau Forest over a length of some 48 km (30 miles) and the location of the Koiwa Fishing

Camp. The Kericho Club has a good 9-hole golf course.

As you leave Kericho on the Nairobi road all the country between you and the Mau is covered with tea for the first 14 km (9 miles) with here and there a tea factory or a group of pluckers in their yellow capes of heavy plastic. They drop the two-leaves-and-a-bud into wicker baskets on their backs, and use long thin canes to ensure that the 'table' remains level.

The Mau Forest comes right down to the edge of the road 41 km (26 miles) from Kericho. After Kedowa, the next landmark 51 km (31 miles) from Kericho is the sign on your left reading 'Londiani—3 km'. Londiani was formerly a station of importance on the railway. Before the line to Eldoret was made and opened in the mid 1920s it was railhead for the Uasin Gishu Plateau and Trans Nzoia; ox wagons would start from here on the long haul to the north through the Tinderet Forest. Londiani is still the site of the Forestry Department's chief training school.

Passing the distinctive hump of Mount Blackett on your right, named after the surveyor who found the present rail route from Nakuru to Kisumu, you climb a long slope to Mau Summit at 2559 metres (8400 feet), where a turn-off to the right leads to Nakuru via Molo. To go straight on here would take you after a few kilometres to the Nakuru-Eldoret road at the junction by the Total petrol station 54 km (34 miles) from Nakuru. This is a slightly faster road, but the route via Molo is scenically more interesting.

Go past Mau Summit Station through a landscape of grassy hills with wheat, sheep, maize, some pyrethrum and plantations and windbreaks of eucalyptus, until you come after 8 km (5 miles) to the Highlands Hotel, Molo. This is a small country hotel much visited by people from Nakuru, and has a sporting 9-hole golf course on a hillside. On your right after Molo township is the turning to upper Molo, a stretch of high wind-swept downland farms. Across the downs and high up on the Mau is Keringet, where wheat was grown on a large scale in early colonial times by Powys Cobb, a well-known Welsh settler who made his own private treaty with the Maasai about 1910. Beyond Keringet and higher up the mountain is Olenguruone, an early settlement scheme for Kikuyu opened to Dorobo settlers during the Mau Mau Emergency.

The next township beyond Molo is Turi, home of St Andrew's Preparatory School; after Turi comes Elburgon. Note the many trestles needed to carry the railway across the ravines of this broken country. Between Elburgon and Njoro there are good views across the Rift. Egerton Agricultural College is on the outskirts of Njoro township, and the road to the south from here leads to the farming district of Mau Narok and over the shoulder of the Mau to Narok in Maasailand. Njoro has a good 9-hole golf course. Straight on through the township takes you by a gentle descent to join the Nakuru-Eldoret road just outside Nakuru, from which it is a two-hour run down the main road to Nairobi.

Places to stay

Nakuru
Stag's Head Hotel
Midland Hotel

Nakuru National Park
Lake Nakuru Lodge
Lion Hill Camp

Eldoret
Sirikwa Hotel
Highlands Inn
New Lincoln
New Wagon Wheel

Eldoret Neighbourhood
Kaptagat Hotel
Soy Club

Kitale
Kitale Hotel

Mount Elgon National Park
Mount Elgon Lodge
Lokitela Farm Guest House

Kakamega
Kakamega Golf Hotel
Kakamega Highway Hotel

Kisumu
Sunset Hotel
New Kisumu Hotel
Lake View Hotel (no restaurant)

Port Victoria
Mulukoba Lakeside Hotel

Bungoma
Bungoma Tourist Hotel

Homa Bay
Homa Bay Hotel
Self-help *bandas* at Lambwe Valley

Kisii
Kisii Hotel
Mwalimu Hotel

Kericho
Tea Hotel

Molo
Highlands Hotel

Mountain walking

Mount Elgon, from Mount Elgon Lodge or Lokitela Farm

Golf

18-hole courses
Nakuru
Kitale

9-hole courses
Gilgil
Eldoret
Soy
Kakamega
Kisumu
Kisii
Nandi Hills
Kericho
Molo
Njoro

Fishing

Gilgil
Malewa River
Turasha River

South Cheranganis
Moiben River

North Cheranganis
Kapolet River (fishing camp)
Chepkaitet River
Morun River

Kericho/Sotik
Apply to Kericho/Sotik Fishing Association, PO Box 281, Kericho for details of temporary membership.
Map of streams along the West Mau Forest edge available at Tea Hotel, Kericho.
Self-help accommodation at Koiwa Fishing Camp convenient for Kipteget, Itare and Kipsonoi Rivers.

Shekhar Mehta, well-known Kenyan rally driver, in the Marlboro Safari

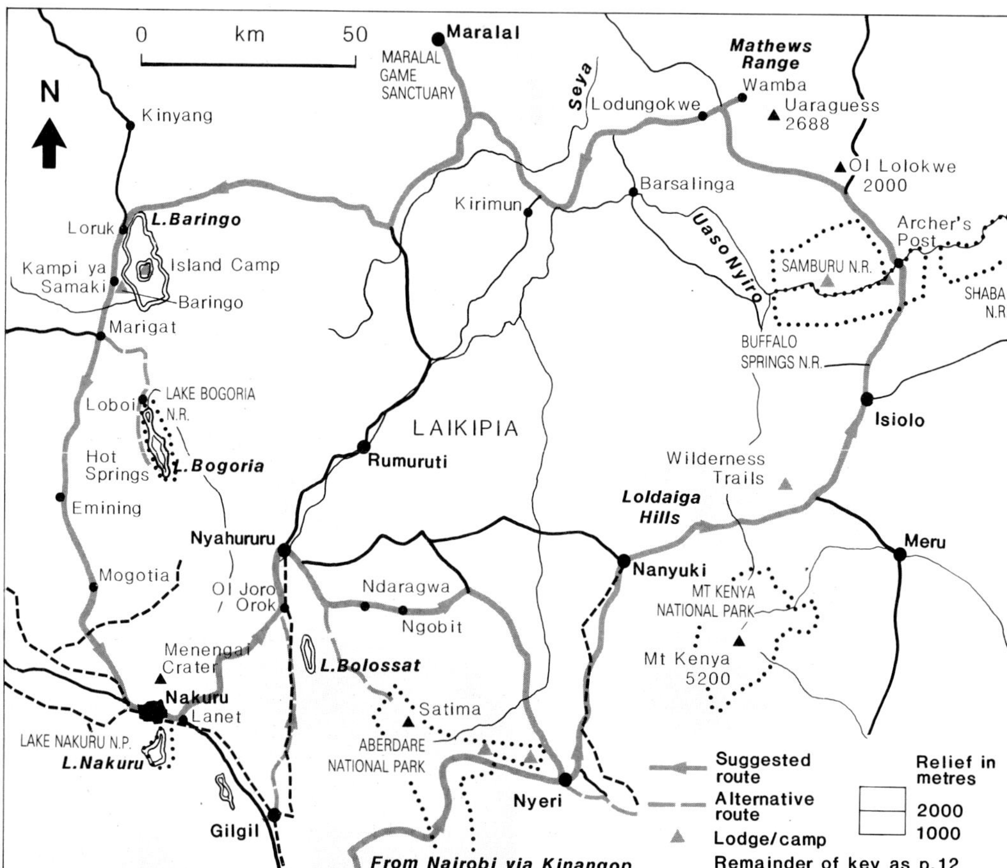

The Rift Valley, Baringo and Laikipia

8 The Rift Valley, Baringo and Laikipia

In central Kenya, north of Nairobi, there are many places within quite easy reach of the capital that are worth a visit. They mostly involve day trips. The kind of longer circuit described in this chapter was made possible a few years ago when with West German assistance a road of good standard was made to link Samburu with Baringo.

The first leg is to Samburu from Nairobi via Nyeri and Nanyuki. You can go as described in Chapter 3, but for a variation why not go to Nyeri via the Aberdare National Park on Nyandarua? Go up the main north road from Nairobi (see Chapter 2), but 3 km (2 miles) short of Naivasha take the road to your right marked 'North Kinangop 24 km'. After you emerge on to the Kinangop plateau the tarmac comes to an end and you fork left for the National Park. This next bit is a dirt road that is often rough and rutted and just has to be endured. However, tarmac begins again well before you enter the forest.

As the country opens out you can see most of the length of the Nyandarua Range from its southern high point of Mt Kinangop 3905 metres (12 816 feet) to the northern high ground of Satima 3997 metres (13 120 feet). The mountain on your left detached from the main range is Kipipiri 3347 metres (10 987 feet). On the far side of this, between it and Satima, is the valley of the Wanjohi River, once a European farming area known as Happy Valley, with a glowing reputation for licentious behaviour, but now the site of a sober and apparently prosperous settlement scheme.

You enter cedar forest, strongly scented with St John's wort, on leaving the plateau at about 2529 metres (8300 feet) and a tarmac road, narrow and twisting but well-graded, then takes you up through the bamboo to the edge of the moorland, where the entrance to the National Park is sited at 3199 metres (10 500 feet). There are brown trout in the streams on top, and a day's fishing licence can be bought at the gate. There is a self-help lodge, Kiandongoro Fishing Lodge, on the Gura River over on the Nyeri side.

The highest trees are the pink- or mauve-flowered *hagenia*, called *mumondo* by the Kikuyu, that you may remember from the Sirimon Track on Mount Kenya. One good main dirt road runs right across the saddle between Satima and the Kinangop, then forks towards the far side, the right-hand road being the shorter and leading down to Nyeri via the Kiandongoro Gate. However, this road has some steep pitches on it and can give trouble after rain. It is better to take the left fork with its longer and gentler descent to the Ruhoruini Gate, with good views down the valleys to the east. As you traverse the park you cross the headwaters of first the Gura and then the Chania Rivers. The Queen's Banda (a visit by Britain's Queen Elizabeth is commemorated) offers a good picnic site with a view of a waterfall on the Chania. There are other picnic and camping sites reached by different tracks leading off the main road, the chief camping area being to the right off the Ruhoruini road after the fork. The sites are high and cold and your water supply may have ice on it in the morning. As for wildlife, there are plenty of elephant and buffalo in the forest and you sometimes see lion out on the moorland. The shy bongo lives in the forest on the Nyeri side, but is very rarely seen from the road. The chances of seeing bongo and leopard are better during a night at the Ark, which lies in the Treetops Salient away to the left on your way down.

There are some kilometres of dirt road after you leave the park, then you strike tarmac again at Ihururu, the village at the foot of Nyeri Hill. It hardly matters whether you turn left or right. Right will lead you round the hill and down into Nyeri past the Outspan Hotel. Left is rather more interesting, since it takes you past Mathari, the Italian mission station. The first Consolata Fathers from Turin arrived here in 1902, and since then there has been a vast expansion. This site has a teachers' college, secondary schools, primary schools, a hospital and a printing press in addition to its church and residential buildings, and round these are hundreds of hectares of good coffee. The mission extended its work to Meru from here in 1911, and still uses Mathari as a base for its operations in the dry country to the north. Just after the mission on your left is a turning to a mausoleum with an avenue of cypresses; this is the mausoleum of the Duke of Aosta, commander-in-chief of the Italian forces in East Africa during the Second World War. At the end of this road, just after the old Masonic Hall, turn right and immediately right again if you wish to cross the Chania into Nyeri town. A left turn here takes you past the Nyeri Inn along Coffee Ridge and across the valley of the Tana, here called the Amboni, to join the main Nairobi-Nanyuki road just past the Police College at Kiganjo.

Proceed as in Chapter 3 to Nanyuki. The left turn at the bottom of the main street leads across Laikipia to Nyahururu. There is a self-service tented camp at El Karama Ranch 42 km (26 miles) to the north-west, pleasantly sited in acacia bush country on the banks of the Uaso Nyiro River. To get there you would turn right at the Naibor signboard 9 km (6 miles) out on the Nyahururu road, go down the Naibor road for 23 km (14 miles) keeping the Nanyuki River on your right, and then turn left when you read 'Ol Jogi—No Shooting'.

Continue out of Nanyuki on the Meru road following the Chapter 3 route, but take the left fork to Isiolo at the bottom of the hill after Kisima. Some 4 km (2.5 miles) from here there is a left turn that leads across Lewa Downs to

Wilderness Trails, a tented camp that provides full services; the 13 km (8 mile) track to the camp is signposted. Your road continues down the long slope to Isiolo, 85 km (53 miles) from Nanyuki. The altitude of Isiolo is 1220 metres (4000 feet), and you are already out of the highlands and at the threshold of the hot dry north. The people here are a cosmopolitan mixture—many Somalis, Meru and Samburu, some Kikuyu, even a small group of Habash (i.e. Abyssinian) traders. There are Christian missions and a rather fine mosque. Camels appear among the livestock. You have to record your departure at the police barrier beyond the town. Then the tarmac ends at a decisive fork—Somalia to the right, Ethiopia straight on.

Go straight on but be prepared for discomfort. The road up through Marsabit to Addis Ababa was up-graded during the 1970s by agreement between the Kenyan and Ethiopian Governments, and a lot of work was done on the Kenya sector by the National Youth Service. But heavy vehicles at speed on gravel-surface roads tend to produce washboard corrugations. The corrugations on this road seem always to be bad, and though you can reduce the vibration by finding an optimum speed, you will still be shaken up.

Relief comes quite soon, since there are four entrances to National Reserves between Isiolo and Archer's Post, 38 km (24 miles) to the north. To the left of the road are the Buffalo Springs National Reserve and Samburu National Reserve, with the Uaso Nyiro River between them. To the right of the road is the Shaba National Reserve.

Burchell's zebra

The game to be seen in this area is varied. There are elephant, buffalo and lion, and the plains game include oryx, eland, impala, Grant's and Thomson's gazelle as well as the Grévy zebra, an animal with narrower stripes than those of the more common Burchell's zebra, and rounded, fluffy, less equine ears. There are no wildebeest—they live only south of the Equator, it seems—but plenty of giraffe, again of a slightly different kind. Those found here are reticulated, and the white lines of their markings form a more sharply defined fishnet pattern than those on the Maasai giraffe found closer to Nairobi. Crocodiles live in the river, and they are often visible from the public rooms of Samburu Lodge on the river's north bank. South of the river and further upstream, beyond the bridge, is the Uaso Nyiro River Lodge; here they put an evening joint of meat in a tree across the river, and a leopard can often be seen when it comes to collect its meal.

At the eastern end of this reserve is Buffalo Springs Tented Camp, also comfortable, with the springs themselves a few kilometres beyond. One rock pool here has been given a paved edge and concrete rim and is clear enough to swim in. Running south from Buffalo Springs to the first gate on the Isiolo road is Champagne Ridge, with several good camp sites. In the Samburu reserve the main camping sites are upstream of the lodge on the north bank of the river. There is no longer any self-help lodge in the area.

Shaba on the other side of the main road was gazetted as a reserve more recently than the other two. It has Shaba Tented Camp on the river's south bank.

When you regain the main road, whether from Shaba or Samburu, head northwards through Archer's Post (named after the Sir Geoffrey Archer who once served here and later governed the Sudan). Around the Post there are usually one or two Samburu *enkangs*, homesteads with a perimeter thorn fence. The next part of this circuit you are doing runs through Samburu country. They are a semi-pastoral people who speak Maasai and have a way of life close to that of the pastoral Maasai of the Rift.

The main road will probably be corrugated and uncomfortable as you head north for the massive hill with a somewhat flattened top called Ol Lolokwe. The countryside is covered with low thorn scrub and the shiny-stemmed *commiphora*, stretching away to distant hills. Just before Ol Lolokwe is reached you turn off the Marsabit road by a turning to the left marked Wamba, and a few kilometres further on the corrugations die down and the road surface improves. You may see a Samburu family on the move with their possessions loaded on to donkeys. As you wind through a low range of hills the forested mountain on your right northwards is Uaraguess, 2687 metres (8820 feet), an outlier of the long Mathews Range still further to the north. Your road circles round to the west of Uaraguess until you come to a T-junction which shows Wamba to the right. Wamba is an administrative and trading centre for Samburu which has a well-

Buffalo in the Mara

equipped mission hospital, but if you wish to pay a visit it means going 13 km (8 miles) off course.

The road to the left at the T-junction takes you over a plain across the Nolgisin stream and through the low Luisie Pass. On your left the hills look like textbook examples of inselbergs. Just before the short rains many of the acacias on these plains are covered with white blossom, and in the bush mauve and blue *ipomeas* are flowering. After passing the turn to Barsalinga and the Lodungokwe shops you come to the hilly country leading up to the plateau from which the Leroghi Forest rises. About 12 km (7.5 miles) beyond Lodungokwe look out for the Lengei Rock, lying like a vast cannonball at the side of the road.

At the edge of the Uaso Nyiro valley the road turns north-west and climbs. The hilly part of this next stretch, the approaches to the Seya River, has a tarmac surface. When you reach the edge of the plateau, 63 km (39 miles) from Wamba, you are half way between Wamba and Maralal and there is a turning to your left marked 'Rumuruti 87 km'.

This track to the left is passable, but has rough patches. As with many roads in ranching country, the surface is quite good on red soil, treacherous on black cotton if at all damp, and like a river bed where a stratum of rock has to be crossed. The first place you come to is Kirimun, a big holding ground where steers from the north used to be mustered before being moved south for slaughter. Beyond this is Colcheccio, a ranch with distinctive yellow gateposts, marked as Soisian on older maps, and from here a signposted left turn will take you back to Nanyuki across the Uaso Nyiro and through the Mukogodo Reserve.

The Dorobo hunter-gatherers of Mukogodo have intermarried with Maasai. The way of life is like that of the Maasai, and Maasai is the main language spoken. A few old people still speak the Mukogodo or Yaaku language, which is Eastern Cushite; but the language has a number of Southern Cushite elements in it from distant times, and this has drawn the attention of linguists. The reserve has a curious dry beauty.

Continuing beyond the junction on the Wamba/Maralal road, you traverse a bare grassy plain that carries both cattle and game, cross the Seya River with the Leroghi Forest to your right, and join the main Rumuruti-Maralal road 91 km (57 miles) north of Rumuruti and 20 km (12.5 miles) south of Maralal. Turn right for Maralal.

As you near the township trees begin to appear near the road. As they get taller and more numerous you realize that Maralal is in the middle of a game sanctuary as well as being the administrative headquarters for Samburu. The township itself is not specially attractive, but about 2 km (1.25 miles) outside it, off the Baragoi road, is Maralal Safari Lodge, a nice cedar-built lodge with well-furnished *bandas*. The verandah of the lodge overlooks a water-hole and salt-lick much visited by game. A drive of 30 km (19 miles) up the road towards Baragoi will reward you with a splendid panoramic view to the north, but venture no further in a saloon car. The country beyond is for 4-wheel drive vehicles, preferably in pairs. As you pass through Maralal you may care to visit the house in which Mzee Jomo Kenyatta spent the last six months of his detention in the years before Independence; it is maintained as a national museum open to the public.

Return down the main Rumuruti road for 54 km (34 miles) and near Mugie Ltd you will see a turning to the right marked 'Baringo 104 km'. This is the second leg of the newly-improved Baringo-Wamba road. As you proceed towards Baringo look out for a group of substantial cairns on your left about 6 km (4 miles) from the Mugie turn-off.

Cairn-building appears to be a common element in the pastoral way of life, usually for burial purposes but sometimes not, and cairns of stones can be found all over Kenya's dry country. We have already come across them at Olorgesailie and in the southern Taru. It is a very old practice, and East African burial cairns are described by one of the Alexandrian grammarians, Agatharcides, in the 2nd century BC. Hamo Sassoon has excavated a cairn at Ngorongoro radiocarbon-dated to the last half of the first millennium BC. These Sukuta Mugie cairns in Samburu are shown on the ordnance survey map in Gothic script, which means that the map maker understood them to be antique, but I have been unable to discover their date.

After about 24 km (15 miles) you reach the edge of the plateau at 1874 metres (6150 feet) and go down the Rift Valley's eastern wall. As you descend there are broad views across the valley to the Tugen Hills and the Elgeyo Escarpment. The altitude is under 1219 metres (4000 feet) at the bottom of the hill, and you are now at the southern end of Pokot country. The Pokot people are partly farmers and partly pastoralists. Those who practise agriculture live up on the slopes of the Cherangani Hills or the sacred mountain of Seger. The cattle herders, who rather look down on their farming cousins, live down on the plains. The women dress mainly in skins still, though some wear cloth dresses; they have bright beaded collars round their necks; the men mostly carry spears and dress their hair with ochre like the Maasai.

The road winds through low hills round the northern end of Lake Baringo, and again the surface changes to tarmac on the steeper gradients. When you reach the cattle holding ground at Loruk, north-east of the lake, you join a tarmac road running northwards up the Rift from Nakuru. Turn left on this, and you will find the left turn to *Kampi ya Samaki* (Fish Camp) about halfway down the lake's western side.

There are three main places catering for visitors to Baringo, and you pass two of them on the road between the turn-off and the little township. The first is Lake Baringo Lodge, an attractive and airy hotel at the water's edge. Second, virtually next door, is the group of pleasant self-help chalets and camping sites

Nanyuki Golf Course, with Mount Kenya in the background

operated by Mrs Betty Roberts. For the third, Island Camp, you have to go to the end of the township and turn right down a track which winds past the pens where Jonathan Leakey used to keep his snakes, to a jetty where you leave your car. A small boat with an outboard engine then ferries you across to Ol Kokwe Island, on the southern tip of which Island Camp is situated; the island is an extinct volcano, and has hot springs at its northern end. At certain times of year it is wise to arrive early at the jetty since storms may blow up in the later afternoon and prevent the boats from running.

The muddy colour of Lake Baringo is due to erosion from the surrounding country; fine particles of dust are held in suspension in the water. The inhabitants of Ol Kokwe Island are Njemps, a people related to the Maasai who live mainly round the eastern and southern shores of the lake. Unlike the Maasai, they are fishermen. They catch their fish mostly close to the lake edge, but they also travel about the lake in canoes propelled by wooden paddles held in each hand. The canoes themselves are made of *ambach* (*aeschynomene elaphroxylon*), a material like balsa-wood. If you want to see *ambach* growing, take the boat trip from Island Camp to see water-birds at the mouth of the Mukutan River; *ambach* is the tree with yellow flowers growing out in the lake; the stems from which the canoes are made are cut under water and have to be dried before use.

Island Camp has its tents skilfully pitched on built-up rocky ledges on a headland. It is well shaded with thorn trees (*acacia tortilis*, the one with seeds like onion-rings). The management have preserved in the sitting-room/bar one feature of interest—a *bao*-board cut in solid rock. *Bao* (a Swahili name) is a game played over much of eastern and central Africa and is also found in Arabia. It is of great antiquity, and has many variations. It is a game for two, played with pebbles in two parallel rows of holes. The aim is for one player to capture the other's pebbles, and the principle is that, on moving round the board, a player by landing in an empty hole on his own side can capture all his opponent's pebbles lying in the hole opposite the one where he stops. Mr David Read, the author of *Barefoot in the Serengeti*, who played *bao* as a boy in Maasailand, says that he has come across boards with 6, 12 and even 24 holes a side. The Island Camp board in fact has 13 holes a side, but Mr Read says this is really a 12-a-side board with two dead holes at the end. The late Louis Leakey gives a full account of the Kikuyu version of the game, with 6 holes a side, in an early autobiography, *White African*. *Bao* boards have also been found at Hyrax Hill, outside Nakuru. If you take an evening walk round Ol Kokwe Island you may come across elderly Njemps actually playing the game, but on a wooden board rather than on carved rock.

As you drive down the main road towards Nakuru, notice the bluff at the southern end of the lake. This is the site of Baringo Fort, built as an outpost from the Eldama Ravine government station in 1897–8 to control the caravan route along which Arab and Swahili ivory-traders were active and were urging the Pokot to resist the administration. The fort was attacked on one occasion by 'seven hundred mixed tribesmen', according to the commandant, but was aided by a relieving force of Njemps warriors armed with spears.

94 km (58 miles) from Nakuru there is a turn-off left to the Lake Bogoria National Reserve. This is by far the best access road to the lake, since the approach road from Mogotio, further south, is rough. A visit is well worth the detour, since Bogoria, a soda lake, has at times great concentrations of flamingoes. You pass through the little village of Loboi and enter the reserve by the Loboi Gate. The track down the west side of the lake is good as far as the two quite impressive clusters of hot springs, but further on it deteriorates. There is a beautiful camp site under trees right at the southern end of the lake, Fig Tree Camp, but the approach road to it at present is vile.

Return to the main road and Marigat, where the road crosses the Perkerra River. The right turn leads to Kabarnet, Baringo District headquarters, where you can stay at the Kabarnet Hotel; the road beyond crosses the Kerio Valley and climbs the escarpment to Tambach and Eldoret.

Your way is south through Emining and Mogotio. About 20 km (12.5 miles) before Nakuru you pass Kabarak High School on your right, the land for which was given by President Moi. Menengai Crater lies to your left as you complete the last few kilometres into Nakuru and join the main road to Nairobi.

Among other places in Laikipia that are well worth a visit is Nyahururu, formerly known as Thomson's Falls. You can reach it from Nakuru by turning left at Lanet, where the road crosses the railway just south of Nakuru, and crossing the high Sabugu ridge to Ol Joro Orok, just south of Nyahururu. You could also reach it by travelling straight down the main road from Maralal through Rumuruti. But perhaps the best route is to make a circuit of Nyandarua by turning off the main Nairobi-Nakuru road at Gilgil, from which a tarmac road leads directly to the town past Lake Ol Bolossat, rich in water birds.

Thomson's Falls Lodge welcomes visitors, and from its garden there is a fine view of the falls, named after Joseph Thomson, the Victorian traveller, who was the first European to see them. Nyahururu is at an altitude of 2346 metres (7700 feet) and is cold at night, but if you stay they will light a log fire in your bedroom. There is a turning off the Ndaragwa road a few miles out of the town which leads up on to Satima, with fine views out over Laikipia and the Rift. It takes you to the northern entrance to the Aberdare National Park, but there is at present no road link through the park to the transverse road you followed at the start of this journey.

The surface is good for your return from Nyahururu via Ndaragwa and Ngobit to Nyeri and so back to town.

Thomson's Falls, Nyahururu

Places to stay

Nyeri
Outspan Hotel
Green Hills Hotel
Central Hotel
White Rhino Hotel
Nyeri Inn

Nanyuki
Mount Kenya Safari Club
New Silverbeck Hotel
Sportsman's Arms

Northern Mount Kenya
Wilderness Trails Tented Camp

Samburu
Samburu Lodge
Uaso Nyiro River Lodge
Buffalo Springs Tented Camp
Shaba Tented Camp

Maralal
Maralal Safari Lodge

Baringo
Lake Baringo Lodge
Mrs Roberts' self-help chalets
Island Camp

Nakuru
Stag's Head Hotel
Midland Hotel

Golf

18-hole course
Nakuru

9-hole courses
Nyeri Club
Nanyuki Club
Mount Kenya Safari Club

Fishing

For facilities around Nyandarua and Mount Kenya, see list in Chapter 3.

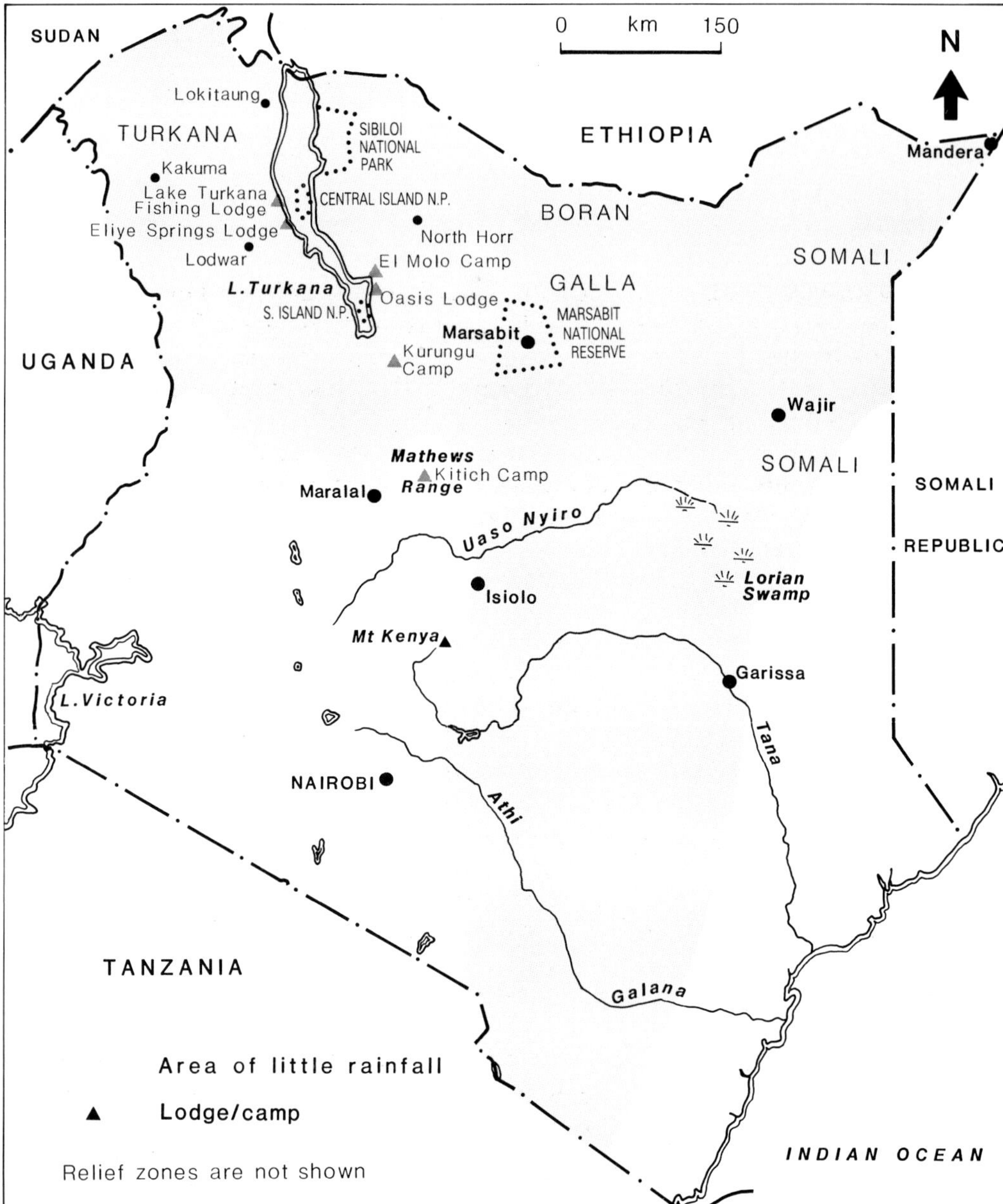

Northern Kenya: the dry country

9 Northern and north-eastern Kenya

Visiting northern and north-eastern Kenya is a rather different kind of travel from what we have so far been considering. Distances are great. There are no towns of any size. Roads are few, rough and largely innocent of garages and filling stations. It is usually very hot during the day. The people of the country are livestock-keeping nomads.

The environment is stark, but much of the landscape round Lake Turkana has a harsh beauty and exerts a fascination on those familiar with it. 'I know of no other place where I would prefer to be', writes Richard Leakey of his fossil-rich wilderness at Koobi Fora on the lake's east side.

If you are to travel at all widely in this part of Kenya you need to be properly equipped. That is, you need to be two vehicles in convoy; the vehicles must be 4-wheel drive; you must carry a lot of fuel and water; you need if possible two spare wheels each, spare fan-belts and hoses, puncture repair kits and patches, a full kit of tools, a tow-rope and preferably a winch as well, plus your food, drink and medical supplies. In other words this country is not to be fooled with. If you get into trouble and have to be rescued you will be unpopular with the administration, who have better things to do.

A road expedition, then, needs quite a lot of advance planning and is expensive. Air travel is an alternative, and indeed all the main places in the north that provide accommodation have their own airstrips, and the charter firms at Wilson Airport frequently take visitors to them. But this is not cheap either. For those who would like a small taste of this part of the world at moderate cost, one sensible plan is to take a week's trip on the Turkana Bus as described below.

The dry lands of Kenya form a vast triangle covering more than half the land surface of the whole country. You may have looked down on this land already from the north slopes of Mount Kenya or the edge of the Leroghi Plateau near Maralal. You have probably passed through the southern tip of the triangle by way of Voi and the Taru Desert. This chapter takes a brief look at its base.

Along the Northern Frontier

What used to be known familiarly in colonial times as the NFD, for Northern Frontier District, is not nowadays a single entity. The north of modern Kenya has three parts, which largely correspond to ethnic divisions.

The land to the west of Lake Turkana is the country of the Turkana people; it is the northern part of the Rift Valley Province, and the district headquarters is at Lodwar. The Turkana themselves are an Eastern Nilotic-speaking group, Nilotes of the plains, who are ethnic cousins to the Maasai and Samburu but less close to their immediate southern neighbours, the Kalenjin-speaking Pokot.

Except for one tiny group of a few hundred fisherfolk living at the south-eastern tip of Lake Turkana, known as El Molo, who are also Eastern Nilotic speakers, the inhabitants of Kenya between Lake Turkana and the Somalia border are Cushites. Those living along the middle section of the northern border and to the south as far as the west bank of the Tana River are Gallas and their relatives, i.e. Kenya's Galla- or Orma-speaking peoples; the main exceptions are the Rendille-speakers, who are related to the Somali. The Galla peoples live in the Eastern Province, and the district headquarters in the northern part is Marsabit.

The eastern section of the northern border and the country southwards as far as the northern fringes of the coastal strip is Somali country. This is the North-Eastern Province, the boundaries of which were fixed to correspond to the recognized boundaries of the grazing areas of the various Somali groups. The Somalis, like the Gallas, are Cushites. Their North-Eastern Province contains three district headquarters, at Garissa, Wajir and Mandera.

Turkana

The country of the Turkana is as arid and inhospitable as any you are likely to see. It is astonishing that 143 000 people should not only survive in it, even if they have to receive recurrent famine relief to do so, but apparently enjoy life fiercely. The men dress simply but have plenty of traditional weapons including spears, wrist-knives and finger-knives. They carry small carved stools which serve as either seat or head-rest, to keep their elaborate coiffure out of the dust. The earth with which the young men dress their hair is blue rather than the red used by cattlemen further south. Lip-plugs and nose-ornaments are worn. The women have finely worked necklaces of beads.

Turkana huts are dome-shaped structures of acacia branches covered with skins and leaves, pitched wherever water and grazing are to be found for their

Camels drinking

animals, and moved from place to place on the backs of donkeys. The people plant what grain and vegetables they can when rain falls to eke out their meat and milk. They also eat fish. The fishermen's co-operative at Kalokol, halfway down the lake's west shore, has become, with years of encouragement from a capable local Fisheries Officer, an established success.

Lokitaung up in the north is where Mzee Jomo Kenyatta spent most of his period of detention in Mau Mau times. It is something of an outpost. Northern Turkana is often in a disturbed state, since raids and counter-raids for cattle across the Uganda border are endemic. From time to time since the days of the Emperor Menelik there have been incursions from Ethiopia. But a development which will do more than anything to bring Turkana into the modern world is now taking place—construction of a proper road link between Kenya and the Sudan. Norway is financing the tarmac to Lodwar; Saudi Arabia is financing a further tarmac stretch to Kakuma; and from Kakuma to Juba a grant from the European Economic Community plus aid from the United States is paying for a high-grade murram road.

A good road to Lodwar will make access easier to the two lodges on the western side of the lake. One is Lake Turkana Fishing Lodge on Ferguson's Gulf; this has good fishing facilities, the chief attraction being the lake's Nile perch, which can be very large, and its tiger fish. The lodge is also a convenient base from which to visit Centre Island, with its three crater lakes. Further south along the western shore is the other centre catering for visitors, Eliye Springs Lodge.

Lake Turkana is the only place in Kenya where there are regular facilities for visitors to fish for Nile perch, though these fish are also in Lake Victoria, to which they are said to have been illicitly introduced some years back. Nairobi's frozen Nile perch packets are now likely to be Lake Victoria fish from Kisumu. Not long ago there was a newspaper report of a Nile perch, caught in a net on the lake, which was so big that it took ten men to lift it on to the top of a bus.

East and south of Lake Turkana

Sibiloi is the name of the National Park on the eastern side of Lake Turkana. Visitors to it these days are interested less in crocodiles than in pre-history, since this is where Richard Leakey and his team have made important discoveries of animal and hominid fossils in recent years. The site is at Koobi Fora—a Gabbra name, this being Gabbra country—and is inside the park. Since the TV series *The Making of Mankind* proved popular there has been growing interest and Koobi Fora has had to reckon with larger numbers of visitors.

There is a small museum there which tells the story of the place and raises revenue for its upkeep. Nearby are some self-help *bandas* where people can stay who have braved the track in Land Rovers and brought all their own food and equipment. You book for these at the National Museum in Nairobi. The easiest access is of course by air.

Towards the south end of the lake, to the north-east of South Island, is Oasis Lodge, a fully equipped lodge in concrete blocks built at Loyengalani near the airstrip about a kilometre or so from the water. Here again the main attraction is fishing. Be careful of the wind in this area. Powerful winds often blow at night and usually die down in the morning. But they can suddenly get up and cause damage. It is thought that this is what caused the deaths of Dyson and Martin, two members of the Fuchs expedition in the mid-thirties who were drowned near South Island.

A few kilometres north of Oasis Lodge is El Molo Camp, a rather simpler affair of wooden cabins which is operated by the company that runs the Turkana Bus.

This bus trip, based on the operator's hunch that people would welcome a journey not so much to see animals or people as primarily to spend a while in beautiful wild country under simple safari conditions, has become quite an institution. At the time of writing it leaves Nairobi every other Saturday morning with its complement of up to 25 passengers and stops for the first night at Maralal. The second night is spent down in the Horr Valley at Kurungu

Camp, also run by the operators of the bus. The third day is rough riding down a series of lava steps to the lake; after a late lunch at the El Molo Camp you are allowed the rest of the day to recover. The fourth day is spent based on the camp with a chance to swim and visit the El Molo. The fifth day is another spell of rugged travel from Loyengalani to a camp at Marsabit. Usually the route is back to the south, then east through the country of the camel-keeping Rendille and the Kaisut Desert to the main Marsabit road; but sometimes the Kaisut is out of action and the bus goes north from Loyengalani to North Horr and then south-east through Gabbra country via the Chalbi Desert to Marsabit. The sixth day is spent having a look at Marsabit and travelling south to the Samburu National Reserve for a night stop. You get back to Nairobi in the late afternoon of the seventh day. That is the normal Turkana Bus trip with transport by fitted truck. The company has also introduced some less basic travel over the same route using Land Cruisers; it costs about twice as much and is called the Turkana Coach.

You may be able to make a separate visit to Marsabit and spend longer there. It would be time well spent, since Marsabit is a remarkable place, a great mountain mass still largely covered in forest rising out of miles of arid plain. The high part, with peaks above 1523 metres (5000 feet), is a National Park and the whole area surrounding it is a National Reserve.

There is adequate rainfall in most years and early morning mist keeps the mountain green. Two crater lakes lie in the forest, the larger of which has a camp site; beside the smaller one is Marsabit Lodge, with all facilities for visitors. There is a variety of game in the park and reserve, but it could not be said to be teeming. Nevertheless there are the beautiful greater kudu to be seen, and the elephants are good: Ahmed, the grand old man who was protected by presidential decree, has now succumbed to old age, but he has a distinguished successor called Abdul.

The 'singing wells' are also worth a visit if you can find a guide to take you there. Here, in wells deep in the rock, men sling up the water containers from ledge to ledge and empty them into troughs at the top to water their stock; while doing so they keep up a rhythmic chant. Please note, by the way, that they prefer not to be photographed while on the job. There are similar wells in other parts of the north and north-east, but those at Marsabit have relatively easy access for visitors.

There is a Marsabit airstrip. There is also a gravelled road from Isiolo, improved some years ago by the National Youth Service. Unfortunately much of it is corrugated and has stony windrows between wheel-tracks, since the soil is such that the gravel will not bond with it.

To the north-east and south-east of Marsabit, in the country between the Nairobi-Addis Ababa road and the boundary of North-Eastern Province, live the Galla Boran. A people closely related to them, the Orma, live further south-east across the Tana River. These peoples, together with the Gabbra and Sakuye, are the southerly part of the big Galla group who used to dominate the north-eastern interior until their decline in the later 19th century. They are related to those Galla who are the main part of the population of southern Ethiopia, but have long been separated from them. In Victorian times the reputation of the Galla was so high that they were regarded as a prime target of missionary endeavour, and it was hoped to convert them and engage them in the spread of Christianity. Krapf in the 1840s had originally planned to work among them, and Charles New, the Methodist, made a journey to their country in 1867. But the Galla were evicted from many of their grazing grounds about this time by the advance of the Somalis and did not fulfil the role for which they had been cast.

The north-east

North-eastern Kenya is Somali country, part of the world of Islam. The Somali population of Kenya is about 375000. They are nomadic stock-keepers, and water and grazing are the main practical considerations in their lives. The little township of Wajir is the hub of the North-eastern Province because of the concentration of wells round it.

At present, unfortunately, it is not possible to recommend a visit to this area of Kenya. For one thing, there are no hotels designed to an overseas visitor's standard. For another, there is a minor security problem. For some time past, on the board in the AA office which reports the state of the roads, there has been a note saying that those travelling from Thika to Garissa, which is the main access road to the north-east, should apply at Mwingi Police Station for an escort because of danger from *shifta*, i.e. bandits.

These bandits are by no means the menace that they once were. Shortly after Kenya became independent, following various violent incidents including the murder of a DC, hostilities broke out in north-eastern Kenya. The war against the *shifta* of 1966–7 was won by the Kenya Army with British troops operating in support; it was won essentially by occupying and holding all the water supplies of the area. Since then the north-east has been comparatively peaceful. However, there are so many guns about in Africa these days because of all the minor wars that such *shifta* as there are find it quite easy to get weapons and so must be taken seriously.

Road travel to the north-east is therefore inadvisable at present, and even for air travel you would be wise to ask police advice and permission. If and when you are encouraged to go, you will find the townships of the province not without interest. At Garissa, apart from the Tana River itself, there is the Boys' Town of the Consolata Mission, started originally to provide a home for

Boran woman weaving thatch for hut.

orphans of the 1966–7 Shifta War. It has become a flourishing community with a great deal of produce, including melons, grown under irrigation from the river. Moyale is where the Nairobi-Addis Ababa road crosses the Ethiopian border. Mandera is at the far north-eastern tip of Kenya; a little agriculture is carried on in the valley of the Daua River here, and in the Rhamu Division of the district there is a Nomadic Boarding School for 240 pupils. Wajir is the most photogenic township, with its square dominated by the white crenellated wall of the prison with the National Flag above. Somali swords are still made in the town, more as curios than for serious use. There is a well established secondary school. The Wajir Yacht Club changed its name after Independence to the Ngamia (Camel) Club, but retained much of its old spirit.

Places to stay

Lake Turkana—west
Lake Turkana Fishing Lodge — Eliye Springs

Lake Turkana—south-east
Oasis Lodge — El Molo Lodge

South Horr
Kurungu Camp

Maralal
Maralal Safari Lodge

Marsabit
Marsabit Lodge

Fishing

Lake Turkana—both from the shore and by boat.

10 Practical matters

Accommodation

If you are on an organized tour to Kenya, where you stay is someone else's problem. If you are going to make your own arrangements you will be wise to make them through a travel agent, since hotels and lodges may get heavily booked except during April, May and June. Your travel agent in your own country can probably provide an introduction to one in Kenya. The two firms in Nairobi with which I have had periodic dealings are Let's Go Travel (PO Box 60342) and Bruce Travel (PO Box 40809), both reliable; there are many more. Let's Go provides its customers with a printed sheet, revised every few months, listing the seasonal rates which are current, for visitors and residents, at nearly 160 hotels, lodges and tented camps. Tented camps are in general no cheaper than lodges; some indeed cost more.

If you are making a long stay it may be worth your while to buy or borrow the equipment which will allow you to use the self-help lodges and *bandas*.

There are cheap hotels in many places where you can rent a room or even a bed for the night; some give you a cup of tea in the morning. These are used quite a lot by young travellers of limited means, and knowledge of them spreads by word of mouth. The favoured ones change frequently and no attempt is made to list them here.

Having made your travel plan, stick to it. Cancellations of rooms booked are not only a nuisance to the innkeepers; they can be expensive for you.

Baksheesh, gratuities, tips etc.

Some restaurants add a service charge to your bill; if so, pay this plus a bit extra. If no service charge is mentioned you are expected to tip; ten per cent of the bill is enough.

Do not tip taxi drivers; instead, agree before you start the journey on what you will pay. If you hire a cab from a reputable firm like Archer's they will tell you what the fare should be. Taxi meters exist but are often out of action.

Some of the beggars on the streets of Nairobi are organized professionals.

Bathing

Beware of sunburn. The sun's rays are fierce on the Equator and an hour or so of carelessly uncovered skin can ruin a week of your holiday or vacation. Break yourself in gently, with limited exposure at first. Note how the locals with fair skins usually wear an old shirt over their shoulders when they go goggling or pottering on the reef. Cloud is no protection, by the way, since the damage is done by ultra-violet rays which penetrate cloud.

For bathing in the sea wear something on your feet as a precaution against stepping on a sea-urchin, which has poisonous spines. You really need an old pair of the kind of rubber shoes called sneakers (US) or plimsolls (UK) or tackies (eastern and southern Africa).

If you graze or scratch yourself on coral treat the wound, however small, with care, since it may easily go septic.

Car hire

Take advice from the Automobile Association (PO Box 40087, Nairobi) on the kind of car that would be most suitable for the sort of tour you are planning. They will probably also be willing to advise you on which of the many car hire firms have a current reputation for reliability. Recently I have heard reports of satisfactory service from Across Africa Safaris, Car Hire Services and Concorde Car Hire. Avis and Hertz are represented here.

Churches, mosques and temples

These in general welcome visitors, although women visitors may not be admitted to mosques in some conservative places. Remember to take off your shoes and make sure you are correctly clothed (i.e. women's arms and legs covered, etc) before entering a mosque. Times of services in Nairobi's Christian churches are normally printed in the newspapers.

Clothes

For daytime wear in Nairobi a light jacket and trousers or a cotton dress or blouse and skirt are adequate for most of the year except June to August, when tweeds and jerseys and woollen skirts are needed. The temperature falls sharply at dusk and warmer clothes can be worn all the year round in the evenings.

On safari the locals usually wear shirts and shorts (men) or shirts and slacks (women). The locally-made safari suits in olive-green or khaki drill are not to be despised; tailors can run them up for you in 48 hours. You must wear something on safari which is cool but will stand up to all the dust and sweat; you then bath at 6.30–7.00 p.m. and change into other clothes for the evening, remembering to protect your ankles against mosquitoes if it's that kind of place. Ordinary Bata safari boots are good footwear.

At the coast you need only the lightest of light clothes—shorts or cotton dresses—throughout the year, with the possible addition of a jersey in July and August. Most people again have a bath about dusk and change into something less informal—long trousers for men—if they are going out; they may just wrap a *kikoi* round themselves if lounging about in the house. (A *kikoi* is a large printed cotton cloth wound round the waist and reaching the ankles, worn as a cool alternative to trousers or skirt.).

Take clothes appropriate to the altitude on your travels, remembering that as a general rule temperatures change by about two degrees Centigrade for every 300 metres (985 feet) of height.

Crime

When it comes to crime Kenya cannot unfortunately be counted among the less developed countries. Our bank-robbers are bold and ingenious, our purse-slitters deft and our con-men silver-tongued. On most weekdays you can see foolish visitors standing in doorways behind the New Stanley, doing illegal currency exchange deals with helpful-sounding strangers.

You can only take the usual sensible precautions—don't carry too much cash, check your insurance, lock valuables in the hotel or lodge safe against a receipt, change money or travellers' cheques only at the official rates in a hotel or bank, and remember to have your passport with you when you do so.

Curios

Wooden Kamba carvings and local batiks are among the easiest to transport. There is also a wide range of good local gemstones, although the quality of the setting varies. Articles carved in Kisii soapstone are attractive but heavy. Banana fibre work is nice but easily damaged. Modern copies of Zanzibar or Lamu brass-studded chests are available, best bought at the coast.

Among the shops offering very fair value are the National Christian Council of Kenya's Cottage Crafts in Nairobi and Tototo Home Industries Centre in Mombasa.

Currency

Take care about declaring what currency you have when you come in so that there are no difficulties in taking out what you have left. Change money only with registered dealers, carrying your passport; exchange rates are printed daily in the press. Don't destroy any remaining Kenya currency notes at the airport when you leave, since it is a criminal offence. On departure, you have to pay your airport tax, at present $10, in foreign currency. Only foreign currency is accepted in the airport's duty-free shop.

Customs

The duty-free import limits are one litre of alcoholic drink and 250 grams of tobacco or equivalent per adult. Any presents you bring are dutiable. Drugs, firearms and pornography are prohibited.

Electricity

The Kenya supply is nominally 240 volts. Some hotels and lodges have adaptors for lower voltages.

Fishing

You must have a licence to fish for trout. You apply for one to the Fisheries Department at PO Box 40241, Nairobi. The cost is reasonable—the fee for a year's licence was raised not long ago from Shs. 40/- to Shs. 100/-, and you can of course get licences for shorter periods. Use fly only and no natural bait. Bag limit for all public waters is six rainbow and four brown trout per day. Although streams are closed or partially closed from time to time, Kenya has no closed season.

Food

The lodges serve normal western European food to the standard of a medium-priced small hotel. The cold buffets are normally well done for lunch; avocado pears are often available, and fresh pawpaw and pineapple are particularly good at the coast.

If you stay in self-help *bandas* you have to take all your own food and drink.

Take pre-cooked stews for main meals, and a variety of canned food. Fridges are not normally available, though the Leopard Rock *bandas* in Meru National Park are equipped with them.

Most of the usual African foods taste fairly insipid to the visitor's palate. Maize flour preparations are the main staple in the agricultural areas. Hardy souls may wish to try the blood and milk mixture of the pastoral peoples. If you want to taste certain kinds of African food, well prepared under good conditions, try the African Heritage Café in Nairobi or the Porini Village Restaurant north of Mtwapa at the coast.

The best guide to local restuarants is Kathy Eldon's *Eating Out in Kenya.*

Health

On entry you no longer need a certificate of vaccination against smallpox. But it is wise to carry a yellow fever certificate, and essential if you have passed en route through an area where yellow fever is endemic. Similarly you need a cholera inoculation certificate if coming from a cholera area.

You should take an anti-malaria prophylactic if visiting the coast, the Lake region or the game parks; remember to start it a week or two before you come and to continue it for a week or two after you leave. (Your doctor should advise you about this.) There is little malaria in Nairobi or at any higher altitude, but some of the diplomatic missions now insist on staff posted to Nairobi protecting themselves against the disease.

Unless you know the particular stretch of water to be safe, avoid bathing in up-country lakes, streams and rivers because of the danger of bilharzia.

Water from the tap is, in general, safe to drink in Nairobi and Mombasa. Elsewhere be careful; one good indicator is whether or not there is a carafe of drinking water in your bedroom.

Sometimes in up-country hotels and lodges the bath water is brown, but this need give no cause for worry.

Sunglasses and a hat are advisable.

In case of accidents in remote places it is not a bad idea to take out temporary membership of the Flying Doctor Service. Some safari firms do this for their clients as a matter of course.

Hunting

Prohibited.

Immigration

You must have a valid passport. In addition travellers from most countries need a Kenya entry visa. This should be applied for at least 30 days prior to travel, either from the local Kenya embassy or consulate if there is one or from a British embassy or consulate if there is not.

At the time of writing entry visas are not required of travellers from these countries: the Commonwealth (except for Australia, Nigeria and British passport holders born in India, Pakistan or Bangladesh), Denmark, Ethiopia, Italy, Norway, Spain, Sweden, Turkey, Uruguay and West Germany. Check your own position now.

On arrival you will have a visitor's pass stamped in your passport for the expected duration of your holiday visit. If you are staying longer than 90 days you will need an alien's registration certificate. If you leave the country and return to it during your visit you will need a re-entry pass from the Immigration Department.

Information

The most informative handbook on up-country conditions is *Welcome to Nairobi* by Anne Chevako and Marjorie Shaver-Jones, published in 1980 and sold in support of the American Women's Association.

Information is available from the Ministry of Tourism, whose headquarters is Utalii House, between the Airways' City Terminal and Uhuru Highway.

The Automobile Association Members' Handbook is useful for motorists.

Three periodicals are of interest: the *Nairobi Handbook*, published monthly, *Tourist's Kenya*, published fortnightly, and *What's On*, a monthly with wide coverage of hotels, restaurants and transport on a national basis.

At Mombasa use the information bureau of the Mombasa and Coast Tourist Association in Moi Avenue.

About fishing, consult the Fisheries Department of the Ministry of the Environment and Natural Resources (PO Box 40241), next to the Museum in Nairobi. See also *Where to Fish in Kenya* by Sylvia Story and Alfred Banner, published in 1976 by Ines May—Publicity.

As for golf, glance through your hotel's stock of publicity leaflets and you will probably find Kenya's thirty courses listed in *Kenya—Golf*, a hand-out of the Ministry of Tourism.

Maps

Maps are quite cheap at the Public Map Office, just behind the President's Office in Harambee Avenue. The best ones for Kenya road travel are the Survey Department's 1:250000 series, but unfortunately some of these have a restricted sale; you have to write a letter to the Survey Department—at the other end of town, next to the Central Police Station—saying which of the restricted sheets you want, and why; armed with this permission, you slog back across town and buy them.

You might make do at first with whatever maps are freely on sale and postpone buying any others until you find yourself at one of the provincial headquarters; outside Nairobi maps are normally sold at the Survey Department's offices, and you will be able to make your case for buying any of the restricted sheets to the officer who can sell them to you.

For central Nairobi, the Esso map and AA street map are good. For Mombasa, the Survey of Kenya's *Mombasa Island and Environs* is recommended.

National institutions

Learn to recognize the Kenya National Anthem, if necessary by going to a cinema and staying till the end. Stand to attention when it is played.

The black, red and green of the National Flag will quickly become familiar. Show it normal respect. In Kenya you are not allowed to photograph the National Flag.

The National Holidays are 1 January, Good Friday and Easter Monday, Labour Day on 1 May, Madaraka Day on 1 June, which celebrates Internal Self-Government in 1963, Idd-ul-Fitr, which comes at the end of Ramadan and so has no fixed date, Kenyatta Day on 20 October, the day of Mzee's arrest in 1952, Jamhuri Day on 12 December, the anniversary of both Independence in 1963 and the declaration of a republic (jamhuri) in 1964, Christmas Day and Boxing Day, i.e. 25 and 26 December.

Photography

As you might expect, photography is big business in Kenya and the general standard of work is quite high. If you are a serious photographer but have never operated in the tropics before you might wander in the camera shops until you find someone knowledgeable to pass on the local wisdom about sun-glare, ultra-violet rays, dust-protection, exposures for dark skins, and so on.

If you are an amateur just wanting a record to take home you will not be short of subjects. But be careful not to photograph military installations or anything sensitive from a security point of view. Forbidden subjects in Kenya are extended to include military personnel and civil prisoners. You may not take pictures of the President or any of his official residences. You may not photograph the Maasai.

Do not openly photograph any people without getting their permission first, and agreeing if necessary on a fee with the commercially minded.

Post

Getting letters and parcels out of the country is not difficult, and the rates are reasonable. Receiving parcels in the country on the other hand is misery and to be avoided if possible; it involves heavy work with the bureaucracy, including customs inspection and the payment of duty and sales tax.

Reference books

For birds, the standard work is the *African Handbook of Birds: Eastern and North-Eastern Africa* (2 vols) by Mackworth Praed and Grant, 2nd edition, published by Longman. The book which people use most on safari is *A Field Guide to the Birds of East Africa* by Williams and Arlott, published by Collins.

For trees, the standard work is *Kenya Trees and Shrubs* by Dale and Greenway, published by Buchanan Plantations, but unfortunately this is out of print and has to be consulted in libraries. There is no field guide to be recommended, though *Trees of Kenya* by J. A. Ojiambo, published by the Kenya Literature Bureau, has a chapter describing some of the common trees.

For snakes there is again no good field guide, though *Snakes and Us* by H. A. Skinner, published by the East African Literature Bureau for children, has clear photographs of some of the snakes you may see.

John Williams' *A Field Guide to the National Parks of East Africa*, published by Collins, is good for learning what the game animals are and where they can be found.

Most of the National Parks and Reserves will sell you a map at the gate which is perfectly adequate for finding your way about and includes a list of the common animals and birds to be seen inside.

If you want to go beyond the phrase-book level in the Swahili language, try Perrott's *Teach Yourself Swahili*, published by Hodder and Stoughton.

Societies

Societies exist in Kenya, nearly all based in Nairobi, that cater for most interests, and some of them, like the Natural History Society and the Geological Society, arrange popular field trips. It would be unwise to try something like climbing the peak of Mount Kenya without contacting the Mountain Club and picking up some local knowledge. *Welcome to Nairobi*, recommended above under Information, contains a useful list of societies and clubs with their addresses. The Natural History Society's bird walk led by Fleur Ngweno that starts from the National Museum in Nairobi at 8.45 a.m. every Wednesday morning is deservedly popular and has become a national institution.

Telephones

The telephone system has had a rapid expansion and can be very temperamental; a heavy fall of rain normally puts many of Nairobi's telephones temporarily out of action. Intermediate distance calls are the hardest to get. Local calls within a single exchange area normally work all right. The service for international calls is good.

Time

Kenya is three hours ahead of Greenwich Mean Time.

Remember that in Swahili, the national language, as in other Bantu languages, the day starts at dawn and ends at dusk, so that *saa moja*, literally one hour, means 7 a.m. or 7 p.m., and one o'clock is *saa saba*, literally seven hours. Unfortunate things have happened because of confusion on this point.

Travel

Air travel is not ruinously expensive; there are regular scheduled services by Kenya Airways from Nairobi to Mombasa, Malindi and Kisumu. Air charter firms operate from Wilson Airport in Nairobi and Moi International Airport in Mombasa. A number are listed in *What's On*.

There are systems of public transport in Nairobi and Mombasa operated by Kenya Bus Services. Various firms including the Overseas Touring Company and Akamba Public Road Services operate the larger buses on the long-distance routes, though many people prefer the smaller vehicles of the Rift

Valley Peugeot Service or Mombasa Peugeot Service. Seats on buses for longer journeys have to be booked in advance.

The *matatu* is an important feature of Kenya road transport. It is normally a converted pick-up or minibus that is licensed to carry passengers, operating at much the same fares as buses on routes all over the country. It is an uncomfortable mode of travel, but an interesting experience; as the saying goes, a *matatu* is never full.

On trains the upper-class berths always need to be booked in advance. Never just turn up in hope at the station. If you miss a train you may have to wait a day or more for the next.

When travelling by road in the dry areas, take not only plenty of drinking water for yourself but some spare bottles as well. If you have to ask for help from the Maasai or other pastoral people there is no more welcome way of thanking them than by a present of some water.

Weather

You can expect dry and warm weather all over Kenya in January, February and March, and these are still the most popular months for visitors, if only because they can avoid the worst of the northern hemisphere's winter.

Gabbra girls and boy herding sheep and goats.

At the end of March the rains normally break. East of the Rift these are the long rains, and they usually last for $2\frac{1}{2}$–3 months, giving place to colder weather that lasts until the end of August. September and October are beautiful months, the equivalent of the northern spring, and they are followed by an interlude of short rains between the latter part of October and mid-December. Things then warm up to the dry season.

West of the Rift the rains continue from April right through to about October, and for parts of western Kenya the wettest month is August. But in a normal year, while eastern Kenya is having its short rains, the dry season in the west has already begun.

Acknowledgements

Warm thanks are due to many people for providing information for this book, notably Peter Robertshaw of the British Institute in Eastern Africa, Harry Merrick of the National Museum, Lorna Hayes of the Mombasa and Coast Tourist Association, Graham Boswell, John Budds, Alan Dixson, Ellen Kitonga, Bill Ndonye, the late John Osogo, Marion Slade, Helen Thuo, Raphael Wesonga, and officers of the Ministry of Tourism and the Ministry of the Environment and Natural Resources. None of them of course has responsibility for any inaccuracies which may remain in the text.

I should also like to thank John Fowler and Matt Cunningham, who visited a number of the rivers and dams mentioned here and reported their experience of the fishing.

Arnold Curtis

Photo acknowledgements

For permission to reproduce photographs, the publishers are grateful to Ardea for pages 49 and 64; John Budds; Hussein Adan Isack for pages 153, 157 and 168; John Jewell for page 86; Marlboro Motorsports for page 136; Vincent Oliver; and Dave Waters for the cover photograph and page 145.